Managing for Accountability

Managing for Accountability

A Business Leader's Toolbox

Lynne Curry

BUSINESS EXPERT PRESS

Leader in applied, concise business books

Managing for Accountability: A Business Leader's Toolbox

Copyright © Lynne Curry, 2022.

Cover design by Charlene Kronstedt

Interior design by Exeter Premedia Services Private Ltd., Chennai, India

First published in 2021 by
Business Expert Press, LLC
222 East 46th Street, New York, NY 10017
www.businessexpertpress.com

ISBN-13: 978-1-63742-074-4 (paperback)
ISBN-13: 978-1-63742-075-1 (e-book)

Business Expert Press Human Resource Management and Organizational Behavior Collection

Collection ISSN: 1946-5637 (print)
Collection ISSN: 1946-5645 (electronic)

First edition: 2021

10 9 8 7 6 5 4 3 2 1

To Ben Swann, the best son I could ever hope for.
To God, who is there with strength, comfort,
and wisdom in every part of my life.

Description

Written by a veteran management consultant, *Managing for Accountability: A Business Leader's Toolbox*, gives business owners and managers a toolbox containing everything they need to hire, inspire, manage, and retain accountable employees who do what they say they will and who invest 100 percent effort into their jobs.

This book is perfect for those who want a roadmap detailing how to: choose exactly the right employee; set expectations for accountability as part of their company culture; inspire employees to "own" their jobs; effectively address problem behaviors that get in the way of maximum performance; retain their top talent; and create accountability in members of Gen X, Y, and Z. Each chapter provides useful, practical, field-tested strategies and solutions that can be immediately implemented.

Written for owners and managers who have little time to read, *Managing for Accountability* is chockful of useful tips and well organized to enable readers to return to specific chapters for a quick reference when they need an immediate tactic or actionable strategy.

The author, a nationally respected organizational consultant and executive coach, offers explicit guidelines for coaching employees to work their hardest to achieve breakthrough levels of performance, maintaining employee commitment at a high level, and bonding employees into high-performance teams united in achieving their employer's business goals and creating an accountability culture.

Readers will find the real-life stories engrossing and the checklists and tools immediately actionable and will walk away knowing exactly how to inspire employees, how to maintain employee commitment at a high level, and how to create an accountability culture in their organization.

Keywords

accountability; productivity; results; employee performance; employee engagement; employee motivation; ownership; retention; employee commitment; buy-in; self-management; all in; discretionary effort

Contents

Advance Reviews

"In Managing for Accountability, Lynne Curry effectively distills 40 years of experience counseling companies across the globe into a practical, step-by-step guide that helps any leader and organization create and sustain a culture of accountability. Curry provides real-life experiences and field-tested solutions to recruit, retain, and inspire high-performing teams. The strategies in Managing for Accountability are useful, simple, and put immediate results within every leader's reach. The book is as enjoyable to read as it is valuable."—**Mark D. Nelson, President and CEO, Bristol Bay Industrial, LLC**

"Managing for Accountability is a top choice in my library of recommended reads. Dr. Lynne Curry has assisted me, my partners, and employees through challenges for more than three decades. She's helped us to work together professionally to achieve our potential, always focused on excellence. She has always been responsive, straightforward, and direct with her meaningful advice and counsel assisting me to develop and grow in leadership."—**Larry Cash, Founder and Chair of the Board, RIM Alaska, California, Guam, Hawaii**

"Managing for Accountability's author is brilliant, inspirational, creative, and brings a fresh and compassionate insight into the workplace. It is a comprehensive and well-written guidebook that every executive, manager, and supervisor will want on their desk. It promotes new ideas for improving employee performance, morale, and the bottom line while creating new cultures. I write this as a business leader with 35 plus years working in the resource and technology industry, government, and the nonprofit sector. This book is a necessary read for management and leaders to succeed in a changing business world, as well as creating future workplace cultures."—**Rebecca Parker, Executive Director of the Anchorage Senior Activity Center**

"In Managing for Accountability, Curry has assembled a collection of lessons learned from her decades of management experience, with lots of strategies and examples that can be applied on a daily basis. This book belongs in every manager's toolbox!"—**Roger Weese, President, Principal, RSA Engineering, Inc.**

"Lynne Curry writes about a topic she has lived with, taught on, and written about every day for many years. In her trainings, I have experienced the depth of her understanding when it comes to people and their relationships to their work. The advice column she produces rivals Dear Abby, except that they are aimed directly at the workplace and how to improve the work environment." —**Mike Coumbe, Deputy Director, Alaska Conservation Foundation**

"I've been following Lynne Curry's superb work as a successful management consultant and coach for over 25 years. Curry's conversational and fast-paced writing style is wonderfully matched with her many pages of important principles for effectively inspiring employees to work harder and as a team fully united toward a common goal."—**Larry Wood, attorney and mediator**

"Managing for Accountability: A Business Leader's Toolbox is a must have for every leader seeking to inspire stellar performance from every employee. Accountability is made, not born and is created, ignited, and fueled by your actions as a leader. Lynne Curry has taken her four decades of human resources expertise and loaded this book with tools for optimizing employees' commitment. This is a must read!"—**Gail Forrest, Senior Human Resources Consultant at Tandem HR**

"Lynne Curry is both an expert in her field and a professional with a knack for breaking challenges down and giving readers roadmaps to help them through difficulties. Managing for Accountability is loaded with valuable information and guidance for becoming a better leader."—**Millie Johnson, Vice President of Shareholder Development at Chugach Alaska Corporation, a company with more than 5,000 employees**

"Lynne Curry's new book drills down to the core of profit, management, and organizational leadership via the relationship between accountability and leadership. The book is a terrific explanation of what accountability means

to an organization and its relationship to profit and leadership."—**Human Resources Attorney Charles Krugel**

"Lynne Curry has identified a key managerial and organization problem and provided practical, achievable, and quantifiable solutions. Creating an organization with accountability from top to bottom and reaping the benefits of a well-functioning team is worth the effort."—**Tom Van Flein, Chief of Staff and General Counsel at the U.S. House of Representatives**

"The key to Lynne Curry's advice is that it is indeed "actionable"."—**Nancy Johnson, Vice President and General Manager, KTUU TV**

"Managing for Accountability's no-nonsense approach to recruiting, hiring, developing, and managing a culture of accountability in the workforce provides today's business leaders with a comprehensive proven toolset." —**Jim Bates, President, LMJ Consulting**

"In Managing for Accountability, Curry has assembled a collection of lessons learned from her decades of management experience, with lots of strategies and examples that can be applied on a daily basis. This book belongs in every manager's toolbox!"—**Roger Weese, President, Principal, RSA Engineering, Inc.**

"Managing for Accountability: A Business Leader's Toolbox has exactly the information and guidance I've been seeking. It's a practical read with a no-nonsense approach. It offers an easy how-to implementation guide for dealing with real on-the-job scenarios. After my first read, I found myself going back to key points I picked up from the book. I was able to execute these tools with employees. Curry delivers her straight-to-the-point professional advice in a way that is easily implementable."—**Brooke McLaughlin, Associate Broker, The Summit Group**

"Curry's Managing for Accountability puts 39 years of management consulting experience into one easy-to-read tool for managers at different levels. Curry's ideas are easy to implement and they deliver measurable results." —**Dee Buchanon, owner, Apex Marketing and Alaska Statewide Director of Marketing, Subway Development, Inc.**

Curry expertly covers how to assess your corporate culture and create a real, effective culture of accountability."—**Todd Clark, President, DenaliTEK**

"This is a clearly written guide to achieving an accountable workplace, one in which managers and employees work for a common goal. Lynne Curry's years of experience have produced a book that will be valuable to any organization."—**Harry Cylinder, CPCU, ARM Risk and Insurance Consultant, Beacon Insurance Services**

"A must read for every business leader. Dr. Lynne Curry provides proven strategies to guarantee your team members are fully vested and committed to your organization's success. It provides solid advice for virtually every situation that business leaders face on a daily basis."—**Paulette Dale, Ph.D, Professor Emeritus, Miami Dade College and Author, Did You Say Something, Susan?**

"Managing for Accountability: A Business Leader's Toolbox fills a long overdue gap in hands-on leadership resources and will elevate the productivity of today's workforce and instill in them a sense of pride and accountability for their work. Dr. Curry's pragmatic approach to accountability and trust translates theory and concepts into a series of carefully considered steps to create an environment where accountability thrives."—**Wilson Duffles, Vice President, Digital Solutions**

"Managing for Accountability offers readers Curry's many years of experience and relays her message with eloquence, knowledge, and a high EQ. I will be the first in line to purchase it for my current and future clients!"—**Debbie Heckendorn, PHR, SHRM CP, President, HR Virtual Partners, LLC**

"Lynne Curry writes a timely book for organizations, managers, and leaders at all levels. Her emphasis on "accountability" underlies the foundation of organizations that seek a well-aligned, competitive team."—**Matt Heilala, President, Alaska Foot and Ankle Specialists**

"Managing for Accountability: A Business Leader's Toolbox is a common sense, tactical guide to better accountability. It's full of things you know or

should know and must do to optimize talent."—**Karen King, President & CEO, Spawn Ideas**

"Lynne Curry's writing style is refreshing and easy to read. Curry lays a great foundation for learning the good, the bad, and the ugly of what accountability is and is not and how to be successful when fostering it. I can't wait to share Managing for Accountability with my leaders."—**Stacy Laackmann, SPHR, Human Resources Director, Northern Valley Health, Inc.**

"Managing for Accountability is for business leaders who are serious about success. Its pages are filled with proven strategies and the practical tools that you've been looking for. Get ready to ignite peak performance that will launch your organization to unprecedented heights."—**Todd Michero, Lead Pastor, Community Covenant Church**

"Managing for Accountability: A Business Leader's Toolbox offers easily found answers to questions every responsible organization should be asking its leadership. For anyone who is looking for specific strategies for an issue or problem, the book is arranged in a manner that lets you go right to the section you need to find an answer quickly. The book is well-written and gives the reader a step-by-step process to help make improvements in employee attitude and work performance. It's a must read!"—**David Morgan, Director, Alaskan Center for Sustainable Healthcare**

"Dr. Lynne Curry's Managing with Accountability inspires you to be a leader with compassion, empathy, and accountability. You will learn strategies to recruit and retain top-performing team members. Using real-world examples, Curry radiates inspirational leadership and helps you create a healthy work culture that motivates your employees to always perform at their best."—**Brenda Pacarro, Workforce and Shareholder Development Supervisor/HR, Calista Corporation**

"A company culture that promotes employee accountability will have a competitive advantage in any market. Lynne Curry's Managing for Accountability: A Business Leader's Toolbox provides business owners and executives with the skills and strategies that will inspire both managers and employees

to be fully committed to and work hard for the company. This book will be a must read if you want to optimize your company's most valuable resource— your employees."—**D. Michael Rabe, Principal/Civil Engineer, CRW Engineering, LLC**

"Lynne Curry has long been recognized as a leading expert in the field of human resources and employee relations. Curry has risen to the difficult task of resolving management/employee issues with a remarkable record of success in getting companies back on track. Managing for Accountability should be a required reading and kept close at hand as a resource to be consulted."—**Attorney William Satterberg**

"Managing for Accountability is a tool every leader and manager will dog-ear and have in the top tray of their toolbox."—**Pat Shier, recipient of the Governor's Denali Award for Individual Leadership and National Cooperative Rx Executive Board Member**

"In Managing for Accountability and in her writing and training, Lynne Curry gives managers, leaders, andemployees practical tools to make the workplace fast-paced, energizing, and a source of rejuvenation."—**Ramji Srinivasan, Founder and CEO at Teiko.bio**

"Managing for Accountability is a must-have, well-written book using relatable experiences that companies can reference to elevate their team's accountability. We can all benefit from Curry's expertise to elevate our HR ROI to 100 percent."—**Gail Stelling, Controller, Arizona Commerce Authority**

"Dr. Lynne Curry has long been the emergency responder for many businesses. We have called Lynne to help us navigate the most challenging moments of growing our business from one to over two thousand employees. When a situation seemed impossibly mired in complexity and negativity, Curry would calmly and professionally chart a path out of the woods for us. In Managing for Accountability, Curry has distilled the lessons of her long career creating solutions from conflict and dysfunction. She is a brilliant communicator who can distill complex strategies and techniques into accessible and

action-oriented language, a skill she has clearly brought to the writing of this book. Business leaders should have this one sitting on their desk for quick reference."—**Dave Stephens, Chief Executive Officer, Ouzinkie Native Corporation and Katmai Government Services**

"Positive. Practical. Succinct. Wise. In Managing for Accountability, Dr. Lynne Curry taps her vast experience to offer a top-notch handbook for those striving to manage with integrity and skill. For quality hires and measurable productivity, this gem of a book is chock-full of insights."—**Award-winning author and former small business owner, Cheryl Bostrom**

"I found Managing for Accountability: A Business Leader's Toolbox insightful. As a leader, I appreciated the steps and questions presented to engage employees to get there."—**Tiffany Van Horn, BU President at Corix Group of Companies**

"This hands-on guide will show you where to focus and what to do to create an engaged, productive culture."—**Wanda T. Wallace, Managing Partner of TheLeadership Forum and Author of You Can't Know It All: Leading in the Age of Deep Expertise**

"Managing for Accountability outlines practical and actionable steps to attract, inspire, and motivate employees to take full responsibility for organizational success."—**Barbara Bell, RurAL CAP, Chief People & Culture Officer**

"Managing for Accountability provides inspiration as well as tangible and effective action steps for leaders to level up their workplace culture to one of accountability. It's a must-read for leaders who are committed to leading from the front."—**Jennifer Woodward, Human Resources Manager, Chickaloon Village Traditional Council.**

Foreword

I am a Fortune 500 General Counsel with experience in labor and employment counseling and litigation for three large organizations across three different industries. I am also the Founder and President of a management consulting firm that focuses on process improvement and resolution of employment disputes.

I have been connected to Lynne Curry for over eight years on LinkedIn and have followed her impressive career during this time. Lynne is an exceptional professional with tremendous expertise in all types of employment matters. Indeed, for 39 years, she led her own training and human resources consulting firm that served over 4,300 clients in 21 states and three countries.

In addition to being the "Dear Abby" of employment law, and publishing weekly advice columns on tricky workplace issues in several states for many years, she is also a successful author of four books on a range of important workplace topics.

Accountability is the key to all corporate success. From a personal level, I pride myself on being an extremely accountable person, ensuring that I always meet my commitments to others. Being accountable has led to increasing levels of responsibility throughout my law firm and in-house career.

From a corporate perspective, accountability is a topic that I am very familiar with, since one of my former employers emphasized it as one of the top competencies needed for success at their organization. To drive this competency to the next level, I was charged with creating an Accountability team in their Legal Department and developing a new process for enhancing accountability in corporate projects.

Once developed, this new process was rolled out broadly and was presented at a Global Legal Conference and shared with other functions within their organization. My positive experience driving accountability within that organization convinced me embedding this competency within any company can be a real game-changer on every level.

Lynne's new book on accountability provides extremely valuable information to help readers like you bring your organization to unprecedented levels of success by teaching you everything you need to know about accountability.

Critical topics covered in this practical toolkit for success include:

- What is accountability, and why it is important for corporate success
- How to determine if your company has an accountable culture and, if not, how to drive a culture of accountability
- How to hire accountable employees, including the specific questions you should ask during interviews
- How to strengthen accountability in new employees and how to coach existing employees to become more accountable
- How to create an accountable environment from the top down using goals, measures, rewards, modeling accountable behavior, and personal connection to employees
- How to create high-functioning teams whose members are accountable to one another
- How to address performance issues by encouraging employees to choose accountability
- How to retain top talent through stay interviews, enhancing trust, providing flexibility, and offering development opportunities
- How a coaching culture enhances accountability
- How to tailor your accountability strategy to be most effective for employees of different generations

In addition, the book includes real-world examples of how accountability concepts and strategies have been successfully applied to companies facing challenges like you face each and every day in your organization.

Because of the importance of this topic and the significant positive impact that enhancing accountability will have on your company's success and bottom line, this is a leadership book well worth reading and adding to your permanent leadership library. I know that I will add it to mine and will refer to this valuable leadership book time and time again in my career.

—Wendy L. Hufford, Founder and President,
Effective Dispute Management, LLC, Rye, NY, 2021

Acknowledgments

Richard Birdsall, J.D., a trusted friend and sounding board who has worked with me for more a decade and has graciously reviewed every concept presented

4,300+ clients who provided thousands of opportunities by offering 43 years of challenges to fix

Wilson Duffles, Vice President of Digital Solutions, Chugach Government Solutions, who pushed me to add new topic areas

Bryan Emmons who created IT sanity, despite COVID-19

Millie Johnson, Vice President of Shareholder Development at Chugach Alaska Corporation, a company with more than 5,000 employees, who encouraged me by saying "I can't wait for this book to be published; it's a roadmap"

Wendy Hufford, Fortune 500 senior vice president, general counsel, and fortune 20 chief litigation counsel, who squeezed reviewing *Managing for Accountability* into her busy schedule

Karen King, President and CEO of Spawn Ideas, whose company ranked nine years in *Outside* magazine's "50 Best Places to Work" in America, who generously squeezed reviewing this book into her fast-paced life

Eric Lincoln Miller, an agent who supports his authors' 100 percent

Subscribers to www.workplacecoachblog.com who field-tested many of the concepts presented in the book now in your hands

Zeke, Deuce, Gracie, and Gabriel who thrust leashes into my hand to encourage "open air thinking" to enhance each day's writing

Other Books by Lynne Curry

Beating the Workplace Bully: A Tactical Guide to Taking Charge by Lynne Curry, AMACOM, 256 pages, 2016

Solutions, Communication Works Inc., 2006 and 2012

Won By One, Communication Works, Inc., 2002

Managing Equally and Legally, McFarland & Company, 1990

CHAPTER 1

What Managing for Accountability: *A Business Leader's Toolbox* Promises You

Accountability is a choice, a decision you want each of your employees to make. Accountable employees demonstrate ownership and take responsibility for results. Employees with accountability invest themselves in your organization; they give 100 percent. They do what they say they will, and more.

Accountable employees ask:

- "How can I contribute?"
- "How can I help my employer, manager, and coworker succeed?"
- "How can I be more productive?"

When you view the inside of an organization staffed by accountable employees, you see employees who:

- Show up on time and ready to work
- Communicate openly and candidly
- Demonstrate reliability
- Work hard
- Admit and learn from their mistakes
- Show initiative and tackle obstacles
- Listen to and act on improvement-oriented feedback

Accountable employees make an owner or executive's work life easier and fuel an organization's success.

Accountable employees also benefit from enhanced professional fulfillment, along with increased respect and recognition from their managers and colleagues.

Making Accountability Happen

Accountability doesn't happen by chance. Although business owners and executives agree that employees can create an organization's competitive advantage, few know exactly how to inspire employees to be "all in," fully invested, and engaged in their work. Creating an accountable organization requires that an owner, executive, and manager make the right choices, take the correct actions, and use finely honed skills and strategies.

In *Managing for Accountability,* you will learn:

- How to recruit employees that give 100 percent effort on the job.
- The clues that tell you a potential hire is someone who takes responsibility for results and demonstrates resilience, even when the going gets tough.
- How to maintain your employee's enthusiasm and commitment at a high level.
- How to inspire employees to show initiative and collaborate with peers.
- How you as a leader can create an accountability culture in your organization.
- How to positively confront and motivate an employee to develop a results-based approach.
- How to build a high-performing, highly accountable team.
- How to retain highly accountable employees who will power your organization to continued success.

Each chapter of *Managing for Accountability* provides you tools, skills, and solutions, along with actionable strategies for maintaining your employees' commitment, excitement, and effort. You will find the chapters chockful of useful tips and well organized to enable you to return to them for a quick reference when you need an immediate tactic.

The net result you will receive from reading and using the strategies presented in *Managing for Accountability*—you will manage employees who are "all in" and do what they say they will—and more. You will gain 100 percent value from your payroll dollars.

Here's your guided tour through the chapters:

In Chapter 2, you will learn what it means to have a workplace in which your employees act with accountability, tackle problems, overcome obstacles, and achieve results. You will understand how accountability starts with you and how your leadership defines a culture of accountability. You will uncover key strategies for assessing and upgrading your workplace culture.

In Chapter 3, you will learn how to attract quality candidates and screen them for accountability. If you have ever hired a lion and discovered you instead on-boarded a kitty, you will learn what to do and what not to do in your future recruitment endeavors when screening and interviewing to avoid unwanted surprises.

In Chapter 4, you will learn strategies and tools for creating accountability and forward momentum in your employees. You will learn how to get your employees aligned and moving in the direction you want. You will learn how to lead your employees to take initiative and to give 100 percent.

In Chapter 5, you will learn how to create an accountability environment in your business. You will gain actionable strategies and tools for creating, increasing, and measuring accountability. You will learn how to use scores, goals, and incentives to incite your employees to win for themselves and your organization.

In Chapter 6, you will learn how to inspire your employees to work harder and as one team, united toward a common goal. You will learn the specific steps that build a high-performance team and how to lead high-energy team events.

In Chapter 7, you will learn how to press the reset button should an employee start to slip. You will learn how to effectively address broken promises, unmet expectations, and other work performance and attitude issues that get in the way of maximum performance.

In Chapter 8, you will learn how to coach your employees, deepening their personal and professional accountability and commitment. You will learn concrete strategies for increasing every employee's commitment, job satisfaction, and connection to your organization's mission and goals.

In Chapter 9, you will learn proven strategies for retaining your best employees and for avoiding the missteps that often lead good employers to lose their best employees.

Chapter 10 focuses on tailoring your accountability management strategies for Gen X, Y, and Z employees, who often don't respond as well to traditional managerial strategies.

How I Can Make These Promises to You?

For 39 years, I ran a nationally respected management consulting company in which all employees aligned with our company's mission and vision. I teach accountability to business owners, executives, managers, and supervisors.

I have directly worked with more than 4,300 organizations in Alaska, Arizona, California, Colorado, Connecticut, Hawaii, Illinois, Michigan, New York, Oregon, Texas, Washington, Washington D.C., China, England, Guam, Japan, and Korea. My clients have included British Petroleum, Conoco Phillips, the U.S. Department of Defense, and the World Bank.

I have qualified in court as an expert witness in the areas of Management Best Practices, Human Resources, and Workplace Issues.

I commit to you an enjoyable read and a book you can learn from. *Managing for Accountability* provides proven strategies and tools you can immediately apply and includes real-world examples that show how these tools and strategies have worked for others and can prove successful for you.[1]

---

[1] Throughout *Managing for Accountability*, "employees" refers to managers and employees.

CHAPTER 2

The Accountability Payoff

In this chapter, you will learn what it means to have a workplace in which your employees act with accountability, tackle problems, overcome obstacles, and achieve results. You will understand how accountability starts with you and how leadership defines a culture of accountability. You will uncover key strategies for assessing and upgrading your workplace culture.

What Accountability Means to You as a Leader, Owner, or Manager

Employees with accountability buy into their organization's mission, own and solve problems, and overcome obstacles.

Accountable employees ask questions such as:

- "What can I do to excel and to add value to the team?"
- "What can I do to solve this problem or fix this situation?"

When your organization has an accountability culture, employees at all levels take responsibility for results and work with 100 percent commitment. As a result, their organizations excel.

What Accountability Is Not

Accountability is not a tool that managers can use to hammer employees with when deadlines are not met, or things go wrong. When leaders use accountability to blame or punish, employees retreat into defensiveness and scramble toward self-preservation or out the company's exit doors.

Clues That Employees Lack Accountability

Employees who lack accountability wait for others to tell them what to do and to fix problems. They blame, complain, finger-point, and lament. Promises are broken, and deadlines get missed. Employees lacking accountability drop balls and deflect responsibility with excuses. As an owner or executive, you hear "it's not my job" or, "don't make such a big deal out of it." Instead of rising above circumstances, these employees react defensively and remain mired in the "not me, not my problem" swamp. Subpar performance becomes the norm.

Does Your Organization Have an Accountability Culture?

Can you tell if your organization has an accountability culture? Yes. Walk into any organization and ask the employees, "what's it like around here?," and you can discover its culture. An employee in one organization says, "I love working here. Everyone helps each other out." At another organization you hear, "You've got to watch your back; it's cutthroat here. And you can't trust the managers."

Every organization of three or more individuals has a culture, a prevalent type of behavior. In some, it is cooperative and collaborative. In others, it is competitive and guarded.

In an organization with an accountability culture, employees demonstrate they are "all in." Employees at all levels hold *themselves* responsible for their actions, behavior, performance, and the results they achieve. Owners and executives can trust employees because when employees say they will do something, they get it done. An accountability culture glues employees together and to their organization.

Productivity and retention rates are high. Employers receive 100 percent value from their payroll dollars. Employees realize their manager, coworker, and organization's success depends on their actions and seek to contribute in ways aligned with organizational goals. They believe that what they do matters. Employees take responsibility for results, and do not assume it is another's responsibility. The baton might pass from one employee to another, but the buck does not.

In an organization lacking an accountability culture:

- The best employees leave for other jobs.
- Employees do not communicate candidly.
- There is little to no sense of urgency about the organization's mission.
- The workplace has more than its fair share of faultfinding, distrust, backstabbing, and blame.
- You hear more negative and defeatist comments than positive, optimistic statements.
- Employees claim to not know what is going on.
- There is an us versus them rift divide between managers and employees.

What if You Need to Upgrade Your Culture?

If your organization's culture needs an upgrade, here is what you need to know. Effort spent on creating a powerful culture pays off. Your organization's culture defines what acceptable manager and employee behaviors are and are not. As a result, organizational culture influences manager and employee actions, and you reap positive or negative results from the culture you create.

A vibrant culture increases manager and employee job satisfaction, morale, retention rates, and productivity. When a culture is positive and solid, profits grow. When a culture is dysfunctional, indifferent, defeatist, or combative, morale and productivity tank.

Your Accountability as a Leader

Accountability starts with you. Leaders shape the organization's culture and need to walk their talk, modeling the ethics and behaviors they want to see in their organization. When an organization's leaders fail to live by the standards they set for employees, the disconnect creates cynicism. If leaders want employees to work with honesty, commitment, and ingenuity, the leaders need to demonstrate integrity, work ethic, and openness to new ideas.

Leaders need to step up to the plate in all areas, starting with outlining a powerful vision of the organization's future and direction. When leaders communicate "here's where we're going and why," it tells the employees that the leader wants employees to own the mission. When leaders communicate upcoming opportunities and challenges and set measurable goals, it creates employee excitement and an attachment to the organization's mission. Openness generates trust. If leaders instead communicate guardedly, holding information close to their vests, employees fill in the gaps with assumptions and speculation. Rumors replace truth.

If owners and executives want their employees to fully invest in their organization, they need to actively engage with their employees, understand their employee's concerns, and solicit employee input. Employees want to have their voices heard and to impact their work environment. Managers who govern from their desks and through closed-door meetings or who only connect via once-and-done employee surveys fall short. An organization's leaders need to open every communication channel and actively interact with employee at all levels. In addition to soliciting feedback, leaders need to listen to and act on what they learn.

Finally, if an organization's leaders value accountability, the organization's policies need to apply to leaders, managers, and all employees. If not, the organization's published code of conduct seems like a bad joke.

Upgrading Your Culture: Action Step One

If you sense your organization's culture needs an upgrade, start with an assessment. Ask yourself and your senior management team questions such as:

- Are we getting 100 percent value from our payroll dollars?
  If we had to establish a baseline for how fully utilized and productive our employees are, what number value would it be?
- What is working well in our organization? What is not working well?
- What do we have to address, change, improve, do more of, less of, start or stop to be even more effective and accountable in the future?

- Are our employees personally invested in their work, or do they just go through the motions?
- On a scale of 0 to 10, how would we, as managers, rate our employees' morale? What number value would they give their morale if we asked them the same question?
- What is getting in our way of making progress as an organization?
- What leads our employees to invest in our organization? What leads them to disengage or leave?
- What are the realities we need to acknowledge about our organization?
- What problems and flaws do we hesitate to talk about (knowing that we cannot begin to solve problems until we admit they exist)?

Self-Assessment

In addition to asking yourself and/or your senior managers the above questions in a group session, train your senior managers and yourself to ask self-assessment and self-reflective questions such as:

- "What have I accomplished today or this week?"; "Am I truly focused on what will enable me to achieve the results I/we seek?"
- "Do I model the behavior I want others to follow? What example do I set for others?"
- How do I make employees feel valued?
- "Where am I/are we ultimately headed and what action steps do I/we need to take to get there?"
- Do I tell it like it is and address facts head on without sugar-coating?
- Am I solution-focused or blame-focused? What would the employees say if asked this question?
- Do I model accountability by admitting my mistakes?
- Am I accessible to my employees, and do I listen to their concerns and suggestions?

- How will I/we evaluate and measure my/our progress?
- Do I clearly and visibly respect all employees, including those who do not agree with me?

Action Step 2: Engage Every Employee in Assessing and Improving Your Culture

Most employees do not initially feel comfortable giving their supervisors, managers, and bosses feedback. If you want to learn and grow yourself, you need to change this.

Here is how—Get in the habit of asking employees what they really think. Ask often enough that they believe you mean it. When they do give you feedback, listen to it, thank them, and act on it.

Ask questions they feel safe to answer, such as "If you were me, what would you prioritize?" or "If you were me, what would you start doing, stop doing, or do differently?"

Increase the amount of feedback you receive by interacting regularly with your employees, inside and outside of regular meetings.

Ask them questions you have asked yourself and other managers, such as "what's working well in our organization and what could be better?" and "what do we as an organization have to address, change, improve, do more of, less of, start or stop to be even more effective and accountable in the future?" My favorite question that I use at the close of every important discussion or interview is "What should I be wise enough to ask you?" Your employees' answers may surprise you and lead you and your organization to continued improvement and growth.

CHAPTER 3

The Tools You Need to Attract Quality Applicants and Screen for Accountability

Selecting the right employees powers your organization's success. In this chapter you will learn:

- Effective recruitment and hiring strategies that enable you to staff your organization with employees who bring accountability to the table
- Recruiting ads that locate and attract the best talent
- How to screen through applicants quickly, effectively, and legally
- Applicant screening and interview strategies that weed out those you do not want and accurately assess what applicants can and will do once hired
- How to identify crucial indications that you have found a candidate who will demonstrate accountability once hired
- Ways to obtain candid reference information from an applicant's former employers concerning how the applicant demonstrated accountability

Writing Standout Ads That Attract Attention

Which ad would attract you, one that makes statements like these: "Our company is one of a kind," "You must demonstrate you can hit the ground running," and "We have very little turnover and want to keep it that way—-or one that read "XYZ Corporation seeks a highly qualified tax accountant to handle a wide diversity of assignments" or "PQR Company needs a top-notch executive assistant for a high demand position"?

If you are a tax accountant, you will likely open XYZ Corporation's ad; however, if the ad reads like a standard job description, you will also circle back to and check out what makes the other employer "one of a kind." You will apply for their job, and also for the position with the employer that reports it has low turnover, guessing that they must treat their employees well.

The bottom line—if you want to attract top talent, write an ad that leads individuals scanning dozens or even hundreds of postings to open your ad.

The NAVAIR recruiting ad (jobs.navair.navy.mil) provides a great example of an ad that attracted thousands of interested applicants (see Figure 3.1 for the ad's full text). It leads with a phrase, "build a career protecting the nation" and includes words such as "challenging" and "exciting." The ad lets applicants discover that NAVAIR offers opportunities in a variety of fields such as engineering, computer science, electronics, finance, logistics, and contract management.

The Naval Air Systems Command (NAVAIR) offers you a challenging and exciting career in the federal government with a variety of opportunities to achieve your career goals. Our work in leading-edge defense systems, engineering, computer science, electronics, and finance, logistics, and contracts management provides our Sailors and Marines with the capabilities they need to accomplish their mission and return home safely.

Figure 3.1 Build a future protecting the nation

How might you attract more job seekers to open your company's ads? Start by creating a list of what makes your company unique, along with the benefits your company provides those who work for it. Ask some of your currently satisfied team members what they most like about your company—you might even gain a few quotes with which to pepper the job postings you place.

Think also about what the most exceptional potential candidates want and do not want in a position and employer. When I created a job announcement for a medical clinic's practice administrator, the third sentence read, "Our five physicians like each other and work well together." The ad pulled hundreds of interested candidates, and more than half of them asked, "Do the physicians actually like each other? I've never worked for a practice where that was true and couldn't pass up your job posting."

When a large, growing company in Anchorage told me they wanted a senior executive for a hard-to-fill position, I included information in the ad about Alaska's hunting, fishing, and hiking options, along with information about the number of flights in and out of Anchorage daily, in order to put to rest some concerns key candidates' family members had expressed about their spouse signing on to a position so far away from extended families.

Finally, make sure your ad operates as a first-level screening tool, causing those without the experience or expertise you seek to realize they need not apply. If you want someone with five or more years' experience in a certain area or individuals with a specific certificate, add one or more lines detailing the required qualifications. This information both dissuades those lacking the needed qualifications and signals to those possessing these requirements that you wrote the ad for them.

Figure 3.2 provides two sample ads, one for an administrative assistant (nonexempt staff position) and one for a clinic administrator (exempt manager position) that produced outstanding results.

Not Just Another Administrative Assistant Position

At XYZ Company, we view the administrative assistant role as key to our company's success.

That is why we are looking for a very special new team member and why we offer unique benefits.

Your office has large windows to the outside, an ergonomic workstation, and a double-monitored computer. Your schedule is flexible, and you can work from home part of the week.

You will join a team of committed, hard-working individuals who like and respect each other.

Here is what we need you to bring to the table—five or more years of highly responsible administrative work; exceptional communications and team skills; experience in managing small company financial records, and high-level expertise in the Office 365 suite.

We pay 100 percent of our employee's health insurance. We provide ongoing opportunities for growth, training, and raises. We offer paid holidays, paid leave starting your first month, and three-week paid personal leave after your second anniversary. We match your contributions in our SIMPLE retirement plan.

To apply confidentially, please submit your resume to _____. You can find our website at _____.

Clinic Administrator

- Would you enjoy the challenge of making both a strategic and a daily difference in Alaska's leading ophthalmic practice?
- Do you have the experience in making a transition into a managed care environment this ophthalmic practice needs?
- Do you have strong people skills and experience in personnel management?
- Do you have experience in financial management?
- Would you like to work for a group of ophthalmologists and opticians who communicate well with each other and with their clinic administrator?

If you answered yes, here is a once-in-a-lifetime opportunity.

Alaska's largest ophthalmic practice [stable and growing since 1972] needs a clinic administrator to handle managed care transition, personnel management, and financial oversight.

If you have people skills, experience in finance, and managed care issues, our physician owners want to meet you.

The successful candidate will:

- Have proven, professional expertise in financial and medical records management
- Possess strong people skills and expertise in all areas of personnel management
- Have knowledge in guiding a clinic through the changes in managed care
- Report directly to the President/Medical Director

If interested, please e-mail us your cover letter and resume to _____. You can also call _____ for more information.

Figure 3.2

Recruiting Strategies That Locate the Best Talent

When you limit your recruiting strategies to placing job announcements on the candidate recruitment sites everyone uses, you will miss some of the best talent—candidates not yet in the job market.

In addition to LinkedIn, Indeed.com, and your company's website, you find the best candidates when you place ads on websites accessed by individuals with the skillsets you seek. This includes professional association websites and newsletters (your state or the national bar association website if you seek an attorney or a senior labor specialist; the Medical Group Medical Management Association if you seek a practice or clinic administrator, the Society for Human Resource Management state or national association website if you seek a senior HR officer, and so forth).

The recruitment sites with the highest applicant traffic include:

LinkedIn Jobs (https://linkedin.com/jobs/search/): The LinkedIn Jobs site accesses both candidates actively looking for a job and those who would explore a good opportunity if it came along.

Indeed.com gives employers access to candidates who have posted their resumes and provides employers the opportunity to post jobs and quickly contact those who have applied.

ZipRecruiter.com allows employers to post a job opening in five minutes.

Jobs.shrm.org provides an example of a site that allows employers to target candidates with a specific expertise (in this case, human resources). Every industry has a similar site.

Finding Applicants Who Are Not Looking for Jobs

The new hire you seek may not be looking for a job. When one of our engineering clients sought an engineering manager with a specialized background, we identified three professional sites that individuals with that specialty turned to. We then sent an announcement to individuals listed as the website's board. Our announcement started, "Unusual opportunity: Do you know an individual who might be interested in" and included information about the job opportunity.

We received 36 resumes, including many from the members of the boards that ran those websites and had impeccable, senior-level qualifications.

Social media and "word of text" (replacing word of mouth) also uncovers and attracts candidates not already on the job market. Ask each of your current team members to advertise your company's position to their connections. When we seek applicants for entry positions, we find many of the best candidates via announcements on Facebook (https://m.facebook.com/jobs as well as on your own posts) and Twitter.

How to Screen Applicants Swiftly, Effectively, and Legally

An effective screening process quickly winnows the number of candidates to a short list of two to five top individuals. As a result, you will be able to spend the time you need, generally a minimum of one to two hours, with each of your top candidates. By investing this time, you will be able to gain an assessment, rather than a quick and potentially false impression of each of them.

Screening Applicants for Accountability: Step One

If you have successfully placed a standout job posting in the right locations, you will face a stack of resumes. You can quickly sort them into "top," "potential," "possibly," and "no" categories if you have first made a list of the criteria most important to you. For example, you may decide to rule out resumes that show rapid "job hopping," those lacking needed experience, or those with grammatical errors on their cover letters or resumes.

Additionally, list the professional attributes you seek, such as "ownership," accountability, initiative, flexibility, adaptability to change, problem-solving, dependability, and empathy, along with those you do not want to see, such as temper, self-righteousness, passivity, and blaming. While these factors may seem intangible, they show up in an applicant's interview answers, past actions at former jobs, and reveal themselves as references describe job candidates.

You can develop your criteria list based on your current and past employees. Once you identify specific criteria, your list becomes a measuring stick you can use when sorting through and interviewing applicants. A fuzzy picture for what your ideal applicant looks like leads to a fuzzy interview and outcome.

Other than sending a quick "thank you, we've received your resume" and "the position has been filled" notice after you have made your selection, you need spend no further time with applicants whose resumes you have rated "no."

Screening Applicants for Accountability: Step Two

Resumes and an applicant's cover letters provide the tip of the iceberg for what you need to learn about a job candidate before going further. Your next step is to send candidates in the top and potential categories a screening questionnaire to gain more information on their strengths and areas of expertise, as well as discovering their levels of accountability and commitment.

Using e-mail screening of applicants saves you time. When you invite candidates to take part in an in-person or video interview, you generally need to spend a minimum of 20 minutes with the applicant so that s/he does not feel brusquely dismissed. If you instead send applicants you have rated as "top" and "potential" a screening questionnaire, you can review their responses in seven minutes per questionnaire, further winnowing your candidate list, enabling you to interview the top two to five finalists rather than eight or more potentially interesting applicants.

A small number of candidates do not respond to the screening questionnaire, and this saves you time, as it speaks volumes about their low interest, energy, and commitment levels.

Figure 3.3 provides a sample screening questionnaire that allowed us to spend four to seven minutes screening though each of 170 resumes for a general manager (GM) position for a startup trucking company. We needed to know:

(a) Which candidates could successfully enable this startup company to grow in a marketplace where cold calling was important?

(b) How the applicants would effectively communicate with and relate to an owner/manager?

(c) Which candidates could describe their fiscal management experience clearly, concisely and in "lay" terms to the owner?

(d) Which applicants understood the nature and duties of the position for which they had applied?

Here are some key questions, along with our rationale for asking each one:

1. "Have you ever cold called a prospect?" Our owner felt that cold calling was necessary in his market. He did not want to hire anyone hesitant to pick up the phone.

2. "If we interviewed the owner/manager you currently report to (or formerly did), what would s/he say about you?" We needed an employee who was willing to communicate openly, honestly, and daily to a hands-on owner.

3. "Please describe your fiscal management experience in budgeting, negotiating, and monitoring costs." Our client owner wanted a highly pragmatic, bottom-line-oriented employee. The owner also wanted someone who was budget-conscious and knew how to negotiate.

4. "What is the longest job you've had and what led you to stay with that job?" Our client owner wanted an employee who would stay for a minimum of 10 years.

5. "How would you describe the role of a GM in serving the owner of a start-up company?" This was the most important question, which is why we listed it toward the end of the e-mail questionnaire. Applicant answers enabled us to rule out one-third of those who sent resumes. Our job posting clearly said that the trucking company consisted of an owner, a bookkeeper, three trucks, and that the GM was expected to drive trucks and grow the company and its market share. Applicants who gave textbook answers concerning a GM's role clearly did not understand the position.

6. "Can you pass a detailed background check, or would we find problems?" We wanted to get this issue out of the way right away. If an applicant could not pass a background check, s/he would not be bondable or able to handle many of the contracts we anticipated.

7. "Please describe how you will go about marketing/selling for a business in the transportation/hauling business." We needed an employee ready to handle the client owner's business challenges on day one.

Based on questionnaire screening, we moved four candidates into phone screening (step three) and two candidates into interviews (step four). We ultimately hired a candidate who had started his own trucking company, sold it, started a second company, sold it to an employee, and later enabled that new owner to sell it, and was interested in moving to eastern Washington, where our client's trucking company was based.

1. What led you to apply for this position?
2. Please describe your background in sales or business:
3. Have you ever cold called a prospect?
4. If we interviewed the owner/manager you currently report to (or formerly did), what would s/he say about you?
5. Please describe your fiscal management experience in budgeting, negotiating, and monitoring costs:
6. What is the longest job you have had and what led you to stay with that job?
7. Please describe your systems for organizing information and follow-through on prospects.
8. How would you describe the role of a GM in serving the owner of a startup company?
9. Can you pass a detailed background check or would we find problems?
10. Please describe how you will go about marketing/selling for a business in the transportation/hauling business.

Thank you for responding to our GM search. We use this questionnaire to select those we will move forward in the selection process. We thank you for your time and ask that you e-mail your answers to (e-mail address).

Figure 3.3 Sample e-mail questionnaire for startup company general manager

Legal Screening and the OUCH Test

When screening applicants, you need to avoid asking discriminatory questions. According to the Equal Employment Opportunity Commission, job candidates are protected against discrimination based on:

1. Race
2. Color
3. Age (40 or older)

4. Gender (sex, including pregnancy, sexual orientation, gender identity)
5. National origin
6. Religion
7. Disabilities
8. Genetic information (including family medical history)

The Uniformed Services Employment and Reemployment Rights Act (USSERA) prohibits discrimination against individuals with present, past, or future military status. Many states and municipalities have additional protected categories enforceable in their jurisdictions. This may include discrimination based on parenthood, marital status, changes in marital status, any age (not just limited to age forty and over), and breastfeeding.

To ensure you pass a legal challenge to your screening process, check with your state's Equal Employment Opportunity (EEO) enforcement agency (an easy Internet search) for the additional categories protected in your state. None of your questions can relate to any of these protected categories.

Questions such as "how would you feel about working for a manager who's younger than you?" would signal that age is on your mind. "How would you feel about having to work with coworkers of a different race?" signals a focus on race, a legally protected category. An interviewer saying, "That's an unusual name; I haven't heard that before" or "that's an interesting accent" might reveal an interest in "national origin," another legally protected category.

OUCH

The OUCH test helps keep you safe. Any question you ask and any job requirement you list must pass all elements of the OUCH test.

OUCH stands for: **o**bjective; **u**niformly applied, **c**onsistent in effect and **h**ave job-relatedness.

Objective requirements and questions zero in on factual matters, such as an applicant's skills, educational background, or experience. Interviewers can translate an applicant's answers to questions covering objective issues into factual, observable, and measurable terms.

A requirement that a candidate needs to have passed the commercial pilot's exam is objective, defines a necessary attribute a successful employee pilot must possess, and does not discriminate against individuals from any legally protected category.

Requiring that a candidate be bondable calls for a specific, factual attribute needed in certain positions and screens out potentially problematic applicants. By contrast, a requirement that an applicant has a warm and friendly attitude is subjective and calls for an opinion, although it might have job-relatedness depending on the position for which you re hiring.

Uniformly applied questions can be asked of every applicant and help you treat all applicants the same, regardless of their protected category. For example, you would not ask an older male "how far along are you," while you may be tempted to ask an obviously pregnant woman that question. If an applicant volunteers that s/he has three children, observing the "uniformly applied" guideline keeps you from asking, "oh, what ages?"

Consistent in effect requirements and interview questions avoid weeding out applicants based on factors related to the legally protected categories such as age, sex, race, religion, and national origin. As an example, the question "Are you willing and able to work overtime?" screens out approximately equal number of applicants in the various protected categories, while the question "Do you have two years of military experience?" screens out more female than male applicants.

Have job-relatedness focuses on requirements necessary for a candidate to be successful in a job. Specific job duties and questions to an applicant must be job-related. For example, a weight or size limit for most positions is not job-related. If the position is for an airline attendant in a small commuter plane, a size limit might be appropriate due to space limitations on the aircraft.

Figure 3.4 Gives you a chance to test your understanding of OUCH's four components

Here's an OUCH self-test; it tests your understanding of the four OUCH components. As you take this brief test, please remember that questions 1 through 4 relate to each letter of OUCH; please ignore the broader question of which items are discriminatory.

1. Which of the following types of information that a job interviewer might notice about an applicant are **objective?**
   a. Excessive hair length
   b. Good attitude
   c. Sex
   d. Marital status
2. Which of the following requirements could be **uniformly applied?**
   a. Do you have a high-school diploma?
   b. Are you willing to work overtime?
   c. All female employees must wear dresses.
   d. All male employees must have short hair.
3. Which of the following requirements are **consistent in effect?**
   a. All applicants must have a history of military experience.
   b. All applicants must have a high-school diploma.
   c. All applicants must weigh at least 120 pounds.
4. Which of the following requirements are probably **job-related?**
   a. Typing skills for a secretary
   b. High school diploma for a shift supervisor
   c. Mechanical ability for a typewriter salesperson.
5. Which of the following pass the full OUCH test?
   a. Management trainees much be under 45 years old.
   b. Truck drivers must be at least 5'6" tall.
   c. Shift supervisors must be willing to work overtime.
   d. A cook must have a positive attitude.

Figure 3.4 Components of OUCH

Here are the answers:

1. "Sex" and "marital status" are objective. An individual is factually male, female, or transitioning. The U.S. census bureau gives us factual definitions for marital status. While sex refers to a legally protected category, it is objective. Although marital status may refer to a legally protected category, it is objective.
2. (a) and (b) can be uniformly applied as they can be asked of or applied to every applicant. Items (c) and (d) are examples of requirements that focus on protected characteristics in the questions themselves.
3. None of these options is consistent in effect; all weed out members of protected categories.
4. Only (a) might be job-related.
5. Only (c) might pass the OUCH test.

Screening Applicants for Accountability: Step Three: Phone Screening

When you are impressed by an applicant's resume and responses to the e-mail questionnaire, you can move to step three—phone screening. If a terrific resume convinces you that you have found an exceptional candidate, you may elect to expedite the process by phone screening an applicant first and letting the applicant know you will be sending an e-mail questionnaire to complete before the in-person interview.

Phone interviews can take 6 to 25 minutes and help you further winnow your applicant list. When you phone the candidates, start by saying, "the next step of the screening process is a short phone interview to ask a few questions. We use your answers, along with your resume and e-mail questionnaire to select those we'll bring in for in-person interviews." By initially announcing that the phone call will be short, you will not risk offending an applicant whose communication patterns or answers lead you to decide not to proceed further.

While on the phone, ask questions such as:

- "What led you to apply for this job?" or "What interests you about this position?"
- "If you had to choose between two jobs and both were offered to you, what would lead you to choose one over the other?"

You can also ask for more detail concerning answers the applicant gave on the e-mail questionnaire.

Phone screening gives you the opportunity to both listen to the content of the applicant's answers and *how* the applicant answers. Does the applicant answer questions directly and concisely or fail to answer the question you have asked or ramble? Do your questions stump the applicant?

If you like what you are hearing, you can continue the phone interview, and also can then schedule the applicant for an in-person or video interview.

Screening Applicants: Step Four: Personal or Video Interviews

To ensure you will be able to assess a candidate, allocate at least an hour for each in-person interview. You may want to interview using a team of two interviewers. When one person asks questions, the second person can observe body language. Team interviewing provides employers multiple other benefits. Not only does each interviewer pick up on different aspects of a candidate's answers, but each interviewer thinks up valuable questions that might not have occurred to the other.

Putting the Applicant at Ease

Start the interview by putting the candidate at ease, whether you are meeting in-person or over Zoom, Skype, or another videoconference medium. Greet the applicant, give your name, and position within your company and let the applicant know you are glad s/he took time for the meeting. Thank the applicant for the materials s/he has already furnished. Smile and then lead off with easy-to-answer questions such as, "I'd like to find out more about your duties in your current/most recent job. Could you outline them for me?"

Arm Yourself with a Question List

A list of 10 to 30 preset questions aids your interviewing effectiveness in five ways:

  a. Your list of preplanned questions ensures you will not forget to ask key questions.

b.   You can review your questions against the OUCH test to ensure you ask lawful questions.

c.   You will not waste interview time trying to think of questions.

d.   Because you have questions prepared, you can fully focus on the applicant.

e.   When you ask the same questions of all applicants, it makes it easier for you to later compare one candidate against the other.

Do not let your list of preplanned questions restrict you. Allow the answers each applicant gives to inspire new questions. Because your candidates bring different backgrounds and experiences to the table, some of which only surface during the interview, you may ask one applicant 70 questions while you ask another applicant only 30.

Take Notes

The notes you record during applicant interviewing prove invaluable if you interview multiple applicants over several days or subsequently face a legal challenge to your hiring decision.

If you interview multiple candidates over time, you may forget what struck or concerned you about an applicant you interviewed five or more days earlier. The specific, factual observations you write in your notes can refresh your memory.

Notes can also end a regulatory agency's challenge to your hiring decision. When I hired a sales manager for one of my clients, Network Business Systems, an investigator from the state's Human Rights Commission called me and said an applicant had filed a discrimination complaint. I faxed the investigator my notes and asked him to read the applicant's response to question #12, "If a customer has an issue with a policy, what will be your first step?" The applicant's response was, "I restate the policy and then explain it." I said, "I won't hire a sales manager who doesn't say, 'I'd first listen to the customer.'" The investigator then ended the investigation.

Watch for Nonverbal Signals

In your interview, watch for nonverbal clues such as matching. Matching refers to the unconscious nonverbal mirroring that occurs between two individuals that instinctively like each other. You have undoubtedly noticed the unconscious mirroring that occurs when one person yawns or smiles, and another yawns or smiles in return.

Because you want your applicant to let his or her guard down and give you honest answers, you will want to initially mirror the candidate. If the candidate then mirrors you, it means s/he possesses good communication skills or feels rapport with you or both. If the candidate does not match you within a few minutes, the lack of matching may signal a lack of connection with you or a lack of good interpersonal skills.

Here is how you can watch this in action. The next time you are in a conversation, notice the similarities between how you and the other person stand or sit, lean, or smile. Then, make a change, perhaps casually raising a hand to your head or altering how you are standing or sitting. If you and the other person have rapport, you will notice the other person making a similar gesture or moving as you move.

Next, the most important nonverbal clues appear as the applicant decides how to answer a question before speaking. These clues are called "meta-expressions." As an example, imagine your applicant tightens their mouth and looks upset but then says, "my supervisor and I got along well." When nonverbal signals contradict what an applicant says, believe the nonverbal.

You may wonder how you can watch for nonverbal signals and simultaneously take notes. If you interview an applicant with a laptop resting on the table between you, you can both watch the applicant and trust your fingers to find the right keys. If you are more comfortable handwriting notes on a legal pad and have always watched the pad as you write, try this experiment. Write several notes on a pad while you are not looking down. You will notice that you can write legibly without looking even though your writing may occasionally veer off the horizontal. You can always transcribe your notes after the interview.

Team interviewing makes it easier to keep detailed notes as well as watch for nonverbal clues. One interviewer can pay close attention to nonverbal signals and take notes, while the other interviewer asks the questions.

Using the "back three jobs" approach to learn "themes"
One of my favorite strategies for quickly learning more about an applicant is by asking about a job or position the applicant held three jobs

prior to their current or most recent position. I ask, "I'd like to learn about your career journey. I'll ask you to travel back in your memories to job X. What led you to take the job?" Once you have heard the answer ask, "What led you to leave it?"

Repeat the process with the position two jobs prior to the candidate's current/most recent job, and then the job prior to their current/most recent position. Take note of any repeated themes. These casually asked questions reveal patterns. You may hear, "I wanted a new challenge" two or three times. If so, you can always ask, "Was there a way you or your employer could have increased the challenges of that job?" You may hear that the applicant left two or more jobs because of a problem supervisor. If so, watch out. If you hire that candidate, you risk becoming a problem supervisor.

Wording Your Questions When You Want the Truth

Your questioning skills have a huge impact on your ability to search out which applicants truly show accountability. To begin, how you word questions plays a key role in getting applicants to speak freely. Questions that begin with "why" or "did" lead applicants to remain guarded. Notice how you react to these questions that seek the same information but start with different words:

> "What puts you in the job market?"
> "What leads you to be interested in this position?"
> versus
> "Why are you looking for a new job?"
> "Why are you interested in this job?"

Here is another set:

> "Why did you decide to leave that job?"
> versus
> "What led you to decide to leave that job?"
> "Why" can place an applicant on the defensive.
> Similarly, "did" leads to shorter answers and can negatively impact the rapport you want between you and your applicant. Compare:
> "Did you prepare budgets?"

"Did you handle stress in your past job?"

with

"What was your experience, if any, with budget preparation?"

"Please describe the amount and type of job stress you experienced in your last position."

You may notice that "did" feels parental, as in "Did you get X done?" versus "What was the status of project X?"

Figure 3.5 provides you a list of sample interview questions. You will notice they often start with "what," "if," and "please." One exception is #11, in which the phrasing "when we call your former supervisor" can gain more truthful answers than "if we call."

Question Timing Strategy and Drilling Down

Most applicants feel, at least initially, on guard. Because of this, you achieve the best interview results when you begin your interviews with easily answered questions and later ask more challenging questions when your applicant has let their guard down. For example, you might start with, "please tell me about your job duties" or "please tell me what led you to start a job search." After hearing the applicant's responses, you can then move on to more searching questions such as:

"If two employers each offered you a position, what factors would lead you to decide to go to work for one employer rather than the other?"

"If you land this job, hoping it will be an 'A' job, what might be the small disappointments that will cause you to feel it is only an 'A–' or 'B+' job after four months have passed?"

"What type of position do you hope to have in two to three years from now?"

"What leads you to want this job rather than another one?"

Once you receive answers to any of these questions, you can drill down to learn more so that you can gain a real assessment of who the applicant is, what motivates him or her in a job, and how likely s/he is to work with one hundred percent commitment.

Sample In-Person Interview Questions

1. What puts you in the job market?
2. What are/were your key duties in your current/most recent job?
3. In the last year, what are two job accomplishments you feel most proud of?
4. If you were offered two jobs, what would lead you to choose one job over the other?
5. If you had to rank order the top three things you are looking for in a good job, what would they be?
6. Please describe what you have liked/disliked about some of your past supervisors.
7. Please describe your experience with working under pressure.
8. If you land this job, where do you hope to be in your career in a year to two years?
9. What are/were the most difficult parts of your current/last job?
10. Please describe your work ethic.
11. When we call your current/former supervisor, what will s/he say about you?
12. If 0 is noncontrolling and 10 is controlling, how would you rate yourself?
13. If 0 is nonjudgmental and 10 is judgmental, how would you rate yourself?
14. Please describe how you took accountability for a handling a situation for your current/former employer.
15. Please describe what accountability means to you.
16. What attracts you to this job?
17. If two employers each offered you a position, what factors would lead you to decide to go to work for one employer rather than the other?
18. If you land this job, hoping it will be an 'A' job, what might be the small disappointments that will cause you to feel it is only an 'A−' or 'B+' job after four months have passed?
19. What type of position do you hope to have in two to three years from now?
20. What leads you to want this job rather than another one?

Figure 3.5 Sample In-person Interview Questions

When you ask unexpected follow-up questions you can move beneath the practiced interviewee's façade. For example, you can ask "Please describe another position for which you have recently applied. What led you to be interested in it? Please tell me two ways in which it is as or more intriguing than our position. Please tell me one reason why our position might be more intriguing to you."

If the answers to your initial questions seem exactly what you are looking for, remind yourself to keep listening with open ears and continue questioning until you have asked every question you consider relevant and feel you have an assessment, rather than an impression, of your job candidate. The time you invest in interviewing can pay off for years.

To make this real, think about the frustration you have encountered with less-than-accountable employees in the past. Let yourself remember the amount of time you spent trying to motivate them and fix problems from the situations they created. Contrast that with the satisfaction you have experienced supervising highly accountable and productive employees. Investing time and effort on the front end saves you time and anguish on the back end.

Questioning that Directly Focuses on Accountability

Include questions that directly focus on accountability and a candidate's sense of responsibility as these questions reveal what an applicant can and will do once hired. Here are some favorites:

> "Please describe your work ethic."
> "Assuming you take this job, what could another employer offer you to woo you away?" (Note: a highly responsible employee will let you know that if s/he is challenged and happy in a job, it will be difficult for another employer to woo him/her away.")
> "What would you consider your responsibility if a coworker becomes suddenly ill?"

You can easily develop other accountability-focused questions by reflecting on what you would want one of your employees to do when faced with a difficult situation. For example, when I interviewed candidates for my consulting company I asked, "You've just taught a class on sexual harassment. As you're packing up your materials an attendee asks you to keep what s/he is about to tell you confidential. You then learn there's an active sexual harassment problem in the organization. How do you handle it?"

The best candidates answer, "Before I let anyone give me confidential information, I let them know that if they give me information that involves illegality, I can't maintain complete confidentiality." They then add, "We have a fiduciary duty to our client when we learn information such as this."

You might ask a manager candidate, "You're the manager of a team in our company. An employee of another team approaches you and asks to speak to you in confidence. The employee describes potential sexual harassment behavior by the supervisor of another team. How would you handle that?" The best candidate's answers parallel the answers above.

Another potential question area that reveals accountability is asking job candidates how they handle a situation in which a coworker complains to them about a supervisor, but then says s/he will not talk to the supervisor because "it won't make a difference." By asking, "What might you say to the coworker?" you learn whether your applicant is someone who coaches his/her coworkers on the importance of maintaining open communication channels with a supervisor or applies another effective problem-resolving strategy.

These types of questions create dialogue between you and the applicant and provide you with valuable information concerning how your potential new employee handles judgment-call situations.

Crucial "Tells" You have Found the Right Employee

When job candidates answer specific "how would you handle…" questions, you can learn whether they will be accountable when it matters most, because accountability shows up most directly when an employee has to reach deep inside to handle an unexpected difficulty.

Here is a real-life example of a highly accountable employee. "Alejandro" was the tour guide hired to take our group of seven to Machu Picchu—except 11 labor unions had just gone on strike in Peru and sought to bring the government to its knees by interfering with tourists.

We had overnighted in Cuzco, waking up at 3 a.m. to get a head start to bypass the strikers, only to discover they had barricaded all major roads between Cuzco and Machu Picchu. Our guide immediately sought information; little was available. He tried seven routes, moving our van quickly on dark streets only to find large boulders and strikers blocking every exit out of the city.

We caucused, and I added my ideas to his. I asked if the outside markings on our van made it apparent that we were American tourists. He did not waver but pulled the markings off and we made it out of Cuzco.

Our troubles were not over. We tried repeatedly to access the Inca trail, but each time found it barricaded and so chose alternate routes. Most buses were honoring the strike. The trains we had hoped to take had been trashed, the windows broken, ties torn off the rails. Our tour guide, who had planned to take us part of the way by train, navigated us onto and off a series of small mountain buses.

We occasionally rented vans. Once after a full day of driving, at 8 p.m. we found ourselves at the outskirts of a community where we planned to spend the night. We were eager to get to our lodging so that we could immediately go to sleep, enabling us to leave at 3 a.m. the next morning. Unfortunately, stalled cars, vans, and buses occupying both lanes blocked the road for more than four miles. The vehicles were not moving. We asked the car ahead of us how long they had been stopped, and they replied, "We haven't moved in at least four hours, maybe more."

Our guide hopped out and spoke to the drivers of five cars parked in the opposite lane. He convinced them all to pull off into a store parking lot. We then pulled into the space they left in the wrong lane, and the vehicles moved back into the lane behind us. Our driver hopped out again and repeated the process. We made it to the place where we slept by midnight. Within the hour, a small caravan of cars followed our lead. By our guide's actions, he changed the lives of those of us in his charge, as well as those of strangers.

The next morning, we inched along the roads to Machu Picchu, heading for the one train that we had understood had escaped the strikers' wrath. When we got there, it was not running. Our guide showed us on a map a back trail we could walk for the rest of the day and into the evening to Machu Picchu.

On normal days, Machu Picchu hosted more than 4,000 visitors. When we arrived, we were eight of less than 100 tourists who made it there.

How? Our guide went above and beyond each day. He problem-solved situations that others did not or could not. He changed the markings on our van, found us a series of buses, inched us through a five-mile-long traffic blockage and led us on back roads. He saw what others viewed as insurmountable obstacles as challenges to be overcome.

Then, when our tour ended, my challenges did not and the guide once again stepped in. Ten days earlier, when I had arrived at LAX to travel to Cuzco, I discovered Bantam Airlines had canceled my flight and routed me on different flight the next day. After the tour ended and I arrived at the Cuzco airport to return to the States, Bantam refused to honor my return reservation because I had not flown my original flight, despite the fact that my original flight had not flown and they had rerouted me.

Although the tour had ended, our guide circled back to the hotel, learned of my predicament, and spent six hours negotiating my way onto another flight. The problem was not his to solve, but he made it his responsibility.

So, how can you tell you have found a candidate who will do as much our guide did? Pose scenario questions, asking "if 'X' happens, what will you do?" The right candidate will signal interest when asked scenario questions. These candidates also ask questions for information, not ones aimed at seeking guidance. Because these candidates thoughtfully and creatively think through situations, they often come up with innovative strategies that may surprise you.

Effective Reference Checking

Effective reference checking gives you crucial information you can gain no other way. The most reliable indicator of future performance is past performance. When we check references, we generally spend 30 to 45 minutes interviewing key references. Figure 3.6 provides you 19 solid reference checking questions you can use.

You may wonder what leads references to stay on the phone for more than a half hour providing reference information. Here is my experience—when I have finished asking the reference my 19 questions, along with other questions that the reference's responses led me to ask, the former supervisor often asks, "Could you send me a copy of those questions?"

1. Can you confirm the dates this individual worked for your company, the position they held, and the reason s/he left your organization?
2. In what situations does this individual excel?
3. What type of supervisor would be the best match for this individual?
4. Please describe how this individual handle conflict situations.
5. What specifically tells you this individual is a good team player?
6. What specifically tells you this individual has good problem-solving skills?
7. How does this individual relate to their supervisor?
8. How does this individual relate to their peers? Do you recall what type of interactions took place?
9. Are you aware of any issues this individual had that might impact job performance?
10. What are this individual's strengths?
11. Every individual has job tasks that they are less effective at. For this individual, which duties did they do least well?
12. What would you say are this individual's Achilles heels?
13. On a scale of 0 to 10, with 10 being highly accountable and 0 being "not as accountable as I would have wanted," how accountable was this employee?
14. Could you tell me a time when this individual took responsibility?
15. Could you tell a time when you wanted this applicant to take responsibility and they did not or did not until it was almost too late?
16. Could you tell me of a time when this applicant demonstrated self-initiative?
17. What appears to motivate this employee?
18. How does this employee handle criticism?
19. Do you have any other comments that would assist us in the selection process?

Figure 3.6 Sample reference questions

You might have heard "former employers don't give references." While that was true 10 to 15 years ago, it is no longer true. Many states, including Alaska, Arizona, Arkansas, California, Delaware, Florida, Georgia, Hawaii, Idaho, Illinois, Indiana, Iowa, Kansas, Kentucky,

Louisiana, Maine, Maryland, New Mexico, North Carolina, North Dakota, Ohio, Oregon, Pennsylvania, Rhode Island, South Carolina, Tennessee, Texas, Utah, Virginia, Washington, Wisconsin, and Wyoming, offer former employers immunity for good faith disclosures of job performance information. If your state is not listed, you can find an updated listing on https://www.nolo.com/legal-encyclopedia/free-books/employee-rights-book/chapter9-6.html.

Because many human resource (HR) departments limit the amount of information that they provide prospective employers, you generally obtain the most substantial and useful reference information from an applicant's supervisors. If you call a supervisor and they say, "I need to route you to our HR department," you can still obtain the supervisor's views by responding, "Thanks, but before you transfer me I have a very interesting question that isn't about the applicant, and that only the supervisor can answer."

After stating this, I always pause, and invariably the supervisor asks, "what question is that?" I ask question #3 from Figure 3.6, worded as "Assuming we hire this employee, what type of supervisor is the best match for them?" My favorite answer was "Mother Teresa."

Even if the HR department limits the information they provide to the basics, the former employee's date of hire, departure, and eligibility for rehire, you may find the information valuable. Employees who have been fired from jobs often leave those jobs off their resumes and fudge the length of prior or subsequent jobs to cover up time gaps.

When you ask an applicant for references, ask for at least three supervisory references. Anyone, even Charles Manson, can come up with favorable personal references.

Finally, Figure 3.7 provides you with a waiver that you can ask your applicant to sign. This waiver, once signed by the candidate, releases former employers from liability for what they say. You can provide it to the applicant's former employers, and it secures reference information from even employers that hesitate to voice negative reference information.

I, _____authorize the release of any and all information related to my past education and training; work records and experience (including skills and abilities); competence; adherence to ethics, integrity and ability to work with others; and my criminal conviction record for the past 10 years, if any. I understand that this information will be kept confidential and only used by XYZ Company to process and document my application for employment. Further, I do hereby release all persons, firms, agencies, or companies from any damages resulting from furnishing such information.

Figure 3.7 Pre-employment release of information form

CHAPTER 4

Creating Accountability and Forward Momentum in Your Employees

In this chapter, you will learn strategies and tools for reinforcing and strengthening accountability and forward momentum in your employees. You will gain effective strategies and tools for getting your employees to give 100 percent effort and align themselves with organizational goals.

Onboarding New Employees

Some owners and executives do not invest time and effort in onboarding their new hires, leaving the process to human resources (HR) departments to orient new team members to organizational rules and to departing employees to detail their replacement's job duties. If this has been your practice, you have taken an easy short-term route that subjects you and your organization to significant long-terms risks.

While many HR professionals project warmth and competency and can provide new-hire paperwork and the personnel policies, they are not the employee's immediate manager. You do not want your new employee's first experience with you to be "hello, see you later," but rather "I'm looking forward to your best efforts and want us to have an open communication channel."

Although your departing employee may be a good person and able to assist your new employee with an understanding of job duties, they may communicate an impression different than how you want your new hire to see the job and you, particularly if he or she is leaving for a "better" job. Not only do you want your new employee to bond with you rather than with your departing employee, but your soon-to-be-former employee may even "poison the well."

At a minimum, you need to spend enough time with your new employee to outline why you hired them, the role you hope he or she plays in your organization, and how you hope the employee will interact with you and the team.

Remember, you want your employee to invest full effort for 40-plus hours a week. Compare this employment investment with the last time you invested a major chunk of money. Before you parted with your money, you asked questions such as, "What will I receive from this investment?"; "What's the upside potential?"; "What downside risks exist?"; and "What do I need to contribute to reap the maximum benefits?"

On your employee's first days and weeks, you need to provide answers to the previous questions if you want to capture your employee's full commitment. You need to explain "here's what we need from you" and here are the benefits.

First-Year Churn and the Bottom Line

In addition to the relationship-building benefits described earlier, effective onboarding makes tangible bottom-line sense. One of the most expensive kinds of turnover any organization faces is "first-year churn" when new hires on whom you have spent time and effort recruiting and training leave before you receive a return on your investment.

Here is how and why this happens. The employee you just hired may receive another enticing job offer after they join your organization. Worse, an unhappy employee on your team may pull your new hire aside and voice concerns. When this happens, most new hires hesitate to let their new employers know what they have heard, both to protect the informant and because they do not want to admit that they listened. Either occurrence may lead to new hire remorse and create festering doubts. Your job is to prove to your new employee that they made the right choice in joining your organization.

Lay the Foundation that Increases New Hires' Commitment

Employers regularly hire me to conduct exit interviews when promising new employees leave within their first six months. After conducting hundreds of interviews, I can document that newly hired employees decide what their employer is like and whether they will fit in and be successful during their first days and weeks.

Recent hires who feel uncertain about their manager, coworkers, job assignments, or own competency begin to think about leaving. They also evaluate minor difficulties negatively, instead of brushing them off.

Counter this downward spiral. Build a strong relationship with your new hires. Integrate them into your team. Provide them with well-thought-out orientation that enables them to perform competently.

The clear expectations you set also align your employees to your business goals and what you need from them. For example, do you want your new exempt employee to realize s/he may often need to give more than 40 hours weekly to his/her new job? Do you expect your new hourly worker to arrive on time every morning and not expect to eat breakfast once they arrive?

In your orientation, outline how you want your employee to communicate with you and how you assess performance. Do you prefer e-mails, texts, or calls? On what topics do you want to be briefed? Do you want your new employee schedule time weekly or to pop into your office whenever they hit a snag? You can also ask your new employee how they hope you will communicate with them.

Figure 4.1 provides you a sample list of expectations you can use to craft your own new hire expectations. I have found the expectations: "treat every client as special and important," "communicate openly, directly," and work a full 40 hours if you are non-exempt, hourly employee, and work 40 to 50 hours if you are an exempt, salaried employee to be particularly important.

What I expect from you:
- Treat every client/customer as special and important
- A high level of communication; communicate openly, directly
  - o Communicate with me directly
    - If you have an issue with me:
  - o Bring it up to me within 24 hours rather than let it fester
  - o Bring it up to me rather than to coworkers
- Good judgment
- Team spirit
- Act in best interest of our company
- Work with enthusiasm and commitment
  - o A full 40 hours if you are nonexempt
  - o 40 to 50 or more hours if you are exempt
  - o Achieve measurable results
- Self-assess your own performance; be committed to your own professional growth and to stellar performance
- Integrity is essential
  - o In client relations
  - o In coworker and employer relations
- Professionalism is crucial
- Cost control is important, including minor costs and maximum benefit from payroll dollars (utilizing your time effectively)

What you can expect from me:
- Honesty
- Professionalism
- Direct communication
- Keep confidences
- Positive and hard working
- Fairness
- Listening
- Open to improvement and will ask for your thoughts
- Leadership
- Commitment to professional and company growth

Figure 4.1 Expectations

Getting Off to a Soaring Beginning
With Your New Employees

When interviewing job candidates, you asked searching questions such as "if you were offered two positions, what would lead you to choose one position over the other?" In addition to placing a copy of your interview notes in your employee's personnel file, use them to start a file on your employee with subheadings such as:

- What motivates (employee)
- What does (employee) hope for from his/her supervisor
- What are (employee's) career goals

In addition to regularly referring to these notes so that you can maintain a high level of enthusiastic accountability in your new employee, continue to update your understanding of what makes and keeps them most productive. Knowing exactly what drives and satisfies each member of your team saves you time, money, and effort, and enables you to focus on providing your team members what they need to feel great about their jobs. Deepen your understanding of what motivates each staff member by occasionally asking questions during their first and subsequent weeks such as:

- "How does the job match up to what you expected when you accepted the position?"
- "What have you found challenging this week?"
- "What have you found motivating this week?"

Figure 4.2 provides you with a script and 11 questions helpful in learning how to keep your new hire at maximum motivation. By asking your employees questions such as these, you engage them in examining their own professional growth and continue to build the bond between you as their manager/coach and them as a fully accountable employee.

Here is a script you can use for holding an effective end-of-week check-in: "Now that you're aboard with us, it's important that I know what motivates you. I'll regularly ask you questions and during this first week or two and may even re-ask questions that you might remember from your hiring interview."

"Your answers may have changed and may continue to change and that's okay; what's important is that I gain and maintain awareness of what motivates you and keeps you at a high level of engagement, accountability, and productivity."

1. In what ways is this job measuring up to what you expected when you accepted our position?
2. What have you found challenging this week?
3. What have you found motivating or satisfying this week?
4. If you had to rank in order the top five things you are looking for in a good job or career, what would they be?
5. What types of job situations keep you most motivated?
6. What types of job situations demotivate you?
7. What part of your job most excites you?
8. Where do you want to be in two years (in your career)?
9. What professional development do you most hope for?
10. Do you have any ideas about how you can improve your engagement, accountability, and productivity?
11. What can I or others do to improve your productivity?

Figure 4.2 End of week one check-ins

Keeping Employees Fully Engaged

Who has the greatest control over the work effort your new hires contribute—you or the employee? If you answered, "the new employee," you answered correctly. Employees control their discretionary effort. This means you need your employees to fully engage from day one and throughout their career with you.

When employees do not fully engage, hard-working owners, executives, and coworkers risk burning out due to work overload, as they compensate for the less engaged employees. Further, your organization spends more in payroll dollars than it receives in effort.

Underutilized employees are far less likely to grow in responsibility and often look outside your organization for new opportunities. While you might think "good riddance" when a low-performer leaves, their departure throws you as an owner/executive into another cycle of recruitment. Two rather than one recruitment cycle costs time and money you will not recover.

Developing a Coaching Relationship

Have you thought about how differently athletes respond to a coach than employees respond to a supervisor? A coach tells a player "hold that ball differently," and the player watches carefully, holds it differently and asks the coach, "have I got it right?" A manager/supervisor tells a direct report, "do that differently," and while many employees answer "certainly," some bristle underneath. While most individuals value a coach, not all employees appreciate being "managed."

Consider what you gain when you establish a coaching relationship with your new team members. Employees who relate to the individual they report to as a coach as well as a manager feel that they and the coach are on the same team. Employees value and work hard for a coach who believes in them.

What makes an employee relate to their manager they report to as if they were a coach? The coaching relationship begins with respect and mutual expectations and is fueled by trust and communication.

Coaches communicate regularly and not only when problems surface. They give pregame pep talks, hold interim time-outs, and meet again at half time. Coaches give immediate, frequent feedback. They debrief players after each major game through objective replays and specifically tell their players how to improve. They let their players know they appreciate excellent performance.

Coaches relate to each employee as an individual. One employee may thrive on starting the day with a list of job duties to perform, while another might find that unacceptable micro-management. You can establish a coaching relationship using the tools already presented in Figures

1. With which of your accomplishments and job duties are you most pleased? [Could you tell me more?]

2. Which of your job duties are you least pleased with? [How come?]

3. How have you improved in performance during the past two months?

4. Are there ways in which I can help you this week?

5. What difficulties or challenges did you have or face during the past two months?

6. What accomplishments have you achieved during this period over and above your standard job description?

7. What aspects of your job do you find most satisfying? Most challenging?

8. What work responsibilities would you like to be handling six months from now? One year from now?

9. What are you learning from your work?

10. What suggestions do you have for making our organization a more satisfying, more accountable or more productive environment in which to work?

11. What action do you feel you or I should take during the coming period to make you more effective?

12. Are there any areas of job challenge or frustration you would like to discuss?

13. What, if any, aspect of your role would you like to change?

14. What are your job goals for the next two months?

15. How do you feel about your current progress toward achieving these goals?

16. How can others or I help you achieve these goals?

17. What should I be wise enough to ask you?

Figure 4.3 Coaching meeting questions

4.1 (expectations) and 4.2 (end of week one check-ins) and then continuing with the 17 "coaching meeting questions" provided in Figure 4.3.

Questions such as "Are there ways in which I can help you this week?"; "What are you learning from your work?"; "What suggestions do you have for making our organization more productive?" let your employee know you are interested in their success and help prevent minor problems from remaining unresolved and festering.

Connecting With All Employees

As an effective leader, you regularly connect with your direct reports. You, your organization, the managers reporting to you, and the employees they supervise can benefit from your planned interactions with all employees.

Here is why: Leaders set the organization's tone and define its culture. When you seize opportunities to be "up front and personal" with all employees, you connect with and inspire them, and model your personal values of integrity and accountability.

You can accomplish this by managing by walking around; maintaining an open door policy; conducting "all hands" and "state of the organization" meetings, and by holding skip-level meetings.

Management by Walking Around ("MBWA")

When you employ "management by walking around" (MBWA) as a regular strategy, you prove that you are an engaged and connected leader personally interested in your employees. You are no longer a distant, unapproachable, intimidating, silent figure behind a closed door and walled off from your employees. You put legs to the importance of direct, open, two-way communication.

MBWA provides you a first-hand perspective on what is going in your organization. As you conduct "walk throughs" and listen and observe, your understanding of employees at all levels leaps forward, and you can spot small problems before they escalate.

MBWA creates a morale lift because it provides you multiple opportunities to recognize good work, show gratitude, and make employees feel you care about them and what they are accomplishing.

When you first begin MBWA, you may have to strike up conversations. You can use the "check-in" interview conversation starters provided in earlier in this chapter, ask questions related to your employee's current projects, or touch base on a situation the employee had earlier shared with you.

In a virtual organization, you can replace your physical walk throughs with a practice of scheduling brief "connection for whatever's on your mind" meetings with each employee.

Maintaining an Open Door Without Undermining Bypassed Managers

By advertising "my door is open" at any time to any employee, you accomplish three key objectives.

You create opportunities for employees to share bold, intrapreneurial ideas with you that might lead to new products or services.

You make "I care about every employee" visible.

You provide an avenue for employees to bring to light hidden problems they might have otherwise taken to individuals or groups outside your organization.

You can easily prevent any problems that might be created by employees who bypass their immediate supervisor when routing concerns to you by asking at the end of conversations, "Have you talked with your manager about this?" and "How can we bring your supervisor in on this?"

All Hands' Meetings

All hands' meetings show respect for employees by keeping them in the know. Regular "state of the organization" briefings conducted by senior leaders or you create excitement, spread the word about recent successes, update employees concerning progress toward the organization's vision and goals, and connect employees throughout the organization with one another.

When you anticipate major changes, you can use a question-and-answer session to give all employees the same information at the same time and respond to questions that otherwise might not be asked. This enables you and your senior management team to surface and resolve employee worries and concerns and to significantly reduce speculation and rumors.

Real-Life Upheavals: How the Question-and-Answer Session Works

Here is how one of my clients used this strategy to handle three major upheavals: a long-term, highly admired CEO's resignation; a well-loved, charismatic CEO's unexpected medically required resignation, and later, the well-respected CEO's untimely death.

Upheaval #1

Employees knew their CEO founder needed to retire but dreaded the idea it might happen. He had founded the company 35 years earlier; many employees had worked for him for decades. They trusted his steady hand at the helm. Many wondered if the company would splinter apart when he left.

They appreciated the four junior partners, but considered them just that, "junior" and occasionally described three of them in less-than-flattering terms. The founder knew this.

When he called me, he explained he wanted to leave "not cold turkey, but I want to turn over the reins."

"In real terms, what does that mean?" I asked.

"I want them to look to the other partners as their leaders, as the men and women running things. I need to turn over the day-to-day running of everything. I don't mind helping the leaders out from time to time, but the employees need to turn to them, not me."

I knew the organization and answered, "That might be a problem. Your employees don't think one of your partners 'leads,' they see him as a follower. Another is younger by decades than many of your employees. They consider him 'wet behind the ears.' Many don't like the third partner."

"I know. So, how do I make this work?"

"Your employees will have fears and concerns that need to be addressed. You need to anticipate what those are and be ready to answer them—all of them. If you do it publicly and everyone hears the same answers at the same time, you'll cut the rumors down."

"You need a method for getting your employees to voice their concerns. And you need a method that spotlights your junior partners' leadership. That will increase everyone's confidence that the company can continue to thrive after your departure."

We agreed on a question-and-answer session, conducted over a long lunch. After everyone had food in front of them, the founder went to the front of the room and said, "I want you to know how much I love and trust you all. Some of you have been with me a long time and you know I won't let you down."

He talked to them about his plan and his faith in the junior partners, talking about each of them specifically. He announced he was making one of the partners the managing partner. He said that while he would be around to answer the partners' questions, he wanted the employees to go to the managing partner and the other three partners with their questions. He told them he would still have a significant financial share in the business and was only transitioning away because he needed more time with his wife and kids.

He had tears in his eyes as did many of his employees. He then waved me to the front and said, he wanted this meeting to be one in which all worries, concerns, and questions were raised and answered, and that he was turning the meeting over to me.

He and the other four partners left the room, and I explained that their founder wanted a confidential way for even the most challenging, hard-to-express concerns to be raised. I asked the employees to move into small groups of two, three, or four, their choice, and said that I would give every group 5 × 7-inch cards on which to write questions, fears, worries, or concerns. I asked that no names be placed on the cards.

"Like what?" one employee asked.

I handed out stacks of cards and said, "Like 'What makes you think you can leave?'; 'What tells you the company can survive your departure?'; 'If we need you later, will you come back?' and, 'Why would you rather play golf than keep working?'" That drew a laugh, and as employees looked at each other, many began to talk and write.

Forty minutes later, the groups handed me their cards, and I visibly shuffled them in front of the group so it no longer appeared obvious which cards had come from which group and announced a break.

When the employees returned, the founder and four partners sat in chairs in front of the group, "This is a reverse firing squad," I announced, and read aloud the first question. The partners took turns answering the questions, with the founder only answering personal ones, and the new managing partner taking the lead in addressing the most challenging questions.

I read the questions without editing, and several hours later, each of the partners in turn committed to leading the company according to the vision and values that they, the founder, and employees believed in. The partners who had received "stinging" rebukes in the questions directed to them vowed to address their weaknesses.

The new managing partner succeeded beyond all expectations. Even more charismatic than the founder, he inspired loyalty and demonstrated integrity, accountability, and compassion toward all employees. The company thrived.

Upheaval #2

Less than two years later, the new managing partner arrived in my office accompanied by his wife. His physician had given him less than two years to live. "My wife and I have always wanted to travel around the world. We've spent the last two months talking about whether I should leave the company or work another six months and prepare our company for another transition."

"Leave. Take care of your health. Travel. Be with your wife and family," I said, tears in my eyes.

"Could we do another of those meetings?" he asked.

"Absolutely."

Only the partners had advance knowledge concerning the topic to be raised at the question-and-answer session. The founder attended, and the look on his and the partners' faces warned the employees bad news was coming. We elected not to combine the meeting with lunch, and to let everyone leave for the day after the partners felt all questions had been answered.

The managing partner addressed the group, telling them his news. He told them how sorry he was to leave them. He told them of his plans to transfer the leadership mantle to one of the other partners, the youngest.

He explained the factors that led him to choose that partner citing the partner's accountability, integrity, work ethic, and commitment. He thanked every employee. Then, he and the founder outlined the guardrails they had put into place to support the organization continuing what had made it strong. He asked every employee to personally commit to helping their coworkers and their company navigate this unexpected transition.

As before, the partner left. I handed out 5 by 7-inch cards. When the partners returned, I read the comments and questions out loud.

The comments, including heartfelt thanks and prayers, outnumbered the questions.

The outgoing and incoming managing partners addressed all questions, occasionally inviting one of the partners to add their thoughts. At the close of the meeting, the incoming managing partner committed to the employees that he would give everything he had to effectively lead the company.

He did. Like the former managing partner, he exceeded expectations as did the employees. The new managing partner and the two other partners worked as a trio to keep the company strong. When the two other partners moved on, the managing partner moved two internal strong performers into junior partner roles. The company continued to thrive.

Upheaval #3

The call came late on a Sunday evening. One of the new junior partners let me know a plane crash had taken the life of the new managing partner. The two partners and I talked, and once again, we held an all-hands' meeting.

At the meeting, the two junior partners told the employees what they knew about the accident and how they planned to navigate the company going forward. The partners tag-teamed each other, each stepping in when the other needed help, their camaraderie obvious. The employees spoke, many through tears. The partners listened and answered the questions that arose. The company had become a family, closely bonded as they came together through adversity.

The company continued to thrive.

Skip-Level Meetings

Skip-level meetings prove invaluable in creating an organization in which employees, the managers under you, and you yourself act with full accountability.

In a skip-level meeting, you connect with the frontline individuals who report to the managers under you. You invite these employees to share thoughts and concerns with you and to ask you questions about anything. In turn, you ask them questions such as the 11 provided in this chapter.

By conducting regular skip-level meetings, you learn what your front-line employees think and feel about your organization and their managers. In skip-level meetings, you step out of your management bubble and discover what you do not hear or see when you live in the good-news cocoon that dilutes bad news before it arrives in your office.

You discover what is really going on beneath the surface. You uncover problems that, while they are not on your radar, need to be before they fester and cost you productivity or employees. For example, you may learn that a significant number of employees disagree with your strategy or do not feel your corporate strategy includes them, or you may hear that a key employee you depend on plans to leave your organization.

Because your frontline employees see customers and clients from a different perspective from you, skip-level meetings offer you insights and improvement-oriented ideas and strategies you would not otherwise have conceived.

Skip-level meetings also demonstrate that you value every one of your employees and want an open, truthful environment. If you are wise, you will make these meetings a regular part of your leadership strategy and your organization's culture.

Implementing Skip-Level Meetings.

Remove the Mystery

Begin by removing the mystery from these meetings, so your "skipped" managers feel comfortable with them and get on board. Explain why you want to conduct the interviews. If they oversee two levels of supervisors and employees, suggest they conduct their own.

Share your intended questions with your managers and ask if they have other questions to suggest. Let them know that you plan meeting with them afterward and will offer them valuable feedback.

A Warm Invite

Create an e-mail inviting a selection of employees to a lunch or breakfast skip-level meeting with you. Here is a potential script for an e-mail:

"I want to make our organization the best it can be. I also want to become the best leader I can be. I'll need your help to achieve these critical goals.

I've decided to initiate skip-level mutual interviews, and you're in my pilot group. Our mutual interview will take approximately forty-five minutes. I'll ask you questions and invite you to ask me any questions you might have, and also to share with me anything you'd like me to know or think about.

Thank you in advance for being willing to participate. If there's anything you say that you want me to keep confidential, I'll honor that, unless it's a legal issue."

The Meeting Itself

Begin the meeting with a statement such as, "Thank you. I realize our mutual interview might feel uncomfortable or even intimidating to you. I realize you might hesitate to say something you think I won't like. I assure you that I'm totally open to whatever you have to say. If I wasn't, I wouldn't schedule these meetings."

Keep your tone warm, friendly, and inviting. Notice the nonverbal clues your employees exhibit that show they are relaxing, such as an open posture, or remaining on guard such as a slight lean away from you. If you are accomplishing these meetings through video conferencing, you may notice an interested or a guarded look in your employee's eyes.

Continue with sentences such as, "I've never wanted be surrounded by *yes* people. I've always wanted to hear from those who see things differently than I do and who are willing to speak truth, like the child in the fairy tale who said, 'Emperor, you have no clothes.'"

If your employee nods, remembering the story, you can continue. If they show puzzlement, you might explain the fairy tale. Then, continue with, "I've always thought it's not the conversations we have that create problems. It's the ones we don't have."

"I'm excited for this interview and I'll start by asking you if there's anything you came here wanting to share with me or any questions you have for me."

Whatever your employee says, listen, without defensiveness or argument. If you do not understand or want your employee to go deeper, ask questions. Take notes; doing so shows respect, that you value your employee's input and take their thoughts seriously.

If your employee asks probing questions, answer them. Do not make your employee feel lesser if they do not open up by sharing something or asking questions. Instead, move forward and ask some of your own, such as the following:

1. What do you enjoy about your job and about working here?
2. What do you think about our company's mission and vision?
3. What do you find unclear about our strategy and vision?
4. If you had all the power, what would you change in our organization?
5. What is one thing we should start, stop, or continue doing as a company?
6. What is the best part of working with your manager?
7. What do you wish your manager would change or do more or less of?
8. What do you do to show accountability?
9. How do you measure success in your job?
10. What can I or our leadership team do to make your career here more satisfying?
11. How do you feel about where the company is going?

Be prepared to be shocked. I still remember a senior manager in one company telling me that in his organization, everyone immediately returned e-mails. I listened while he told me that the overloaded, ready-to-crack middle manager I had coached needed to stop trying to do so much herself. "All she has to is tell someone she needs help."

He clearly lived on a different planet. My coaching client and others had told me the organization did not operate as he described. Many senior- and mid-level managers did not return e-mails to employees for days, if at all. According to the overwhelmed middle-level manager, not only did others not offer help but instead they insisted she perform work, for which they later claimed credit.

The senior manager lived full-time in a high-level management bubble and had no clue why so many in his organization continued to resign.

After asking questions, you can again ask if your employee has questions for you or has anything to share with you. Thank your employee for the gift of candor they have given you and the organization. Ask what you may share with their manager.

After the meeting, honor what your employee has told you by sending a follow-up e-mail, thanking them again and adding any specific follow-up notes you feel are important.

Job Reviews: A Tool to Keep Employees Moving Forward in the Direction You Want

If you were managing a football team, would you hold your feedback until the end of the season? Why then wait until the end of the year to deliver a performance review?

Like postgame coaching, a job review becomes a valuable tool for enhancing productivity, accountability, and alignment with overall business goals. Informal job reviews conducted every three to four months take 20 minutes or less and pay off in huge productivity and accountability benefits.

Here is how to conduct an effective informal job review. Provide these five questions to your employee a day to a week before you conduct the review:

1. What do you see as your role?
2. In the last three months, what have been your greatest accomplishments?
3. If you were your own supervisor/manager, what would you tell yourself you needed to work on?
4. How can I or others in our organization help you be more productive?
5. What goals do you have in mind for the next three months)?

_____   _____
Employee's signature   Today's Date

When you meet for the review, ask your employee for their answers to those five questions. Listen, take notes, and respond to what you have heard. Then give your own feedback and resolve any differences.

With question #2, you acknowledge your employee's hard work and initiative. Because question #2 leads you to compliment your employee, it smooths the way to discussing problem areas in question #3.

Question #4 outlines how you or others can help your employee. Your employee may have asked for specific types of support or told you that what you are already doing is what s/he needs.

Question #5 moves you and your employee forward. When you provide your employee your thoughts, you can outline the areas in which you want your employee to take initiative and provide new, additional effort.

Figure 4.4 provides you with additional questions you can ask during the review. I have found question #1, "How can you build on the success you have had?" valuable for creating a high level of motivation and accountability and for leading employees to take a higher level of initiative.

---

1. How can you build on the success you have had?
2. What results have you produced that please you the most?
3. What have you learned?
4. What accomplishments have you achieved above and beyond your key responsibilities?
5. Which aspects of your job do you find most satisfying?
6. What suggestions do you have for making our organization a more engaging, accountable, and productive place to work?
7. What skills or capabilities would you like to develop to improve in your current role?
8. In what areas do you want to grow to better achieve your professional or career goals?

Figure 4.4 Additional questions you can ask during the review

CHAPTER 5

Creating an Accountability Environment

In this chapter, you will learn how to create an accountability environment in your organization that supports productivity and performance. Creating an accountability environment that achieves outstanding bottom-line results requires that you to know how to (a) establish purpose, (b) set goals, and (c) define a scorekeeping system. You will gain tools and actionable strategies for creating, measuring, and increasing accountability, and learn the art of using goals, scores, and nonmonetary incentives to incentivize your employees to win for themselves and your organization.

Leaders Define the Accountability Environment

As a leader, you define the accountability environment. Employee accountability rests on each employee's understanding of his or her role in achieving clearly articulated organizational objectives. When your employees know the results that they need to accomplish and why their actions matter, they become attached to your organization and willingly take ownership and give extra effort.

Here is an example for how this works, even if you do not presently manage a team of already-accountable employees.

Giving Employees a Common Purpose Inspires Buy-In

When I took over as an executive director for an organization called Kuyana House, Inc. in Nome, Alaska, the suicide rate in Nome was 44 times national average. Those at highest risk were young people between 13 and 21 years old. Drug and alcohol abuse were rampant.

I staffed the center with seven teenage peer counselors. I picked young people who appeared to be natural leaders, even though six of them had, at that time, alcohol and drug problems themselves. After providing them two weeks of intensive training as counselors, I asked them, "Who's committed to wiping out suicide in Nome?"

"What do you mean?" one asked.

"Taking suicide to zero."

"Is that even possible?" another asked.

"Yes," I answered, knowing that every one of my seven employees had lost a family member or close friend to suicide. I watched shock and hope splash across their faces. Then I asked, "If we're going to do that, what do we need to do ourselves?"

We brainstormed, and I listed the ideas on a white board. Initially my staff offered predictable answers, including "continued training, hiring more staff, and public service announcements." Then, one young woman nicknamed "Bugs" said, "We need to get off drugs ourselves."

After another five minutes of brainstorming, I handed every team member a marker and asked them to put a star by the item on the list most likely to help us meet our goal. "We need to get off drugs ourselves" won the most stars.

"When do you start?" I asked. The teens looked at each other. It was not easy, but none of them touched drugs after that night. Accountability created: I had set the scene; they had chosen a goal; they had bought in. As a leader, I had done what you can learn to do—I had created the "hook" that caught my team's attention and interacted with my employees in a dialogue rather than a monologue.

A postscript—suicide dropped to zero in Nome and remained at zero for the next three years, and I left to run a statewide training network to show other counseling centers how to accomplish similar results.

Communicating the "Why"

When leaders explain "this is why we're doing this," it accomplishes multiple purposes.

The effort and time you spend engaging employees in understanding your vision for your organization shows you value them as key contributors. When employees know "why" and feel your organization's purpose important, it creates excitement, boosts morale, and inspires personal effort and ownership.

Knowing the end goal transforms what your employees do in the same way that getting the football across the goal line changes running full out across the field fifty times in practice from "I have to" into "I want to do this so we can win."

"Why," often described as an organization's vision and mission, brings to mind the story of the passerby who asked two bricklayers, "What are you doing?" One answered, "laying bricks," and the other responded, "building a cathedral." Which bricklayer do you think worked harder and with more motivation?

Are You Ready to Talk "Why"?

You will know you are ready to talk "why" if you can answer these questions yourself:

- Why is our organization and its mission important?
- Do I have passion for what we need to achieve, and can I explain it in ways that will achieve others' buy-in?
- What is it about our organization's purpose that will engage our employees' minds and hearts?
- What difference will our organization and/or its products and services make to our clients or customers?
- Why now?
- If our organization did not exist, what will be missed?
- Why are we the best team to accomplish our organization's mission?

How will you know your employees have bought in?

- If your employees buy-in to the purpose, you will hear, see, and feel it.
- You will see your employees fully engaged, working productively, and going above and beyond minimum expectations.

- You will hear your employees talking about your organization's purpose to others.
- Your employees will show resourcefulness when confronting obstacles.
- Your employees will passionately express their enthusiasm for realizing your organization's vision.

The Bottom-Line Value of Goals

Have you ever thought about how hard many individuals work when involved in sports or recreation? Or wondered how it is that employees who find it hard to concentrate at work focus intensely when playing baseball? Or found it interesting that employees who drag themselves into the office at eight manage to wake at 4 a.m. on Saturday to head for their favorite fishing hole? What is it about sports and recreational activities that motivate individuals to apply their maximum effort?

If you answered "goals" or "winning," you correctly identified two variables you can instill in your organization to keep employee excitement and accountability high. Consider goals such as "win the game," "beat your previous time," "bat above the .400 mark," "catch your limit," "run a 5-minute mile," or "make a score." In sports and recreation, clearly defined goals allow individuals to win and to celebrate their accomplishments.

When basketball, soccer, or football players run back and forth across the gym or field during practice sessions, they do not run to run. They run so when it counts in a game, they can run fast enough to make a basket or score a goal or touchdown. If it were not for personal goals, would 30,000 people wait two predawn hours on the chilly Brooklyn Bridge to run 26 miles with "Boston Strong" blazoned across their tee shirts? Goals translate "here's why we're doing this work" into "this is exactly how we'll know we've scored a win." Business owners and executives ignite employee energy when they incorporate goals into their organization's life.

"Win the Game" Goal-Setting Made Simple

You can set organizational, departmental, or team goals in two ways.

You as the owner or executive can establish them, or you can involve your team in setting goals. Either way works. Both approaches follow the same process. The difference—how many individuals do you involve in goal-setting?

In most private sector organizations, senior management establishes the goals and involve employees at all levels in determining how to implement those goals.

In nonprofit organizations, the board of directors and senior managers establish goals and priorities in an annual strategic planning session. The board then turns those goals over to the management team to create and implement detailed plans, and then report back on the organization's progress.

Here is your five-step goal-setting process:

Step 1: Establish or review your mission or purpose. If you choose, you can also establish a vision and corporate values.

Step 2: Review your organization's baseline information:
- What is going right?
- What is your strategic analysis of your past success and failures?
- What is your organization's financial capacity?
- What are your organization's other resources and limits?
- What are your organization and team's strengths?
- What problems do you and does your organization need to address?

Step 3: Look at your organization from the outside in:
- Who are your organization's primary customers and clients that purchase or benefit from your products or services? What are the criteria by which they would assess your organization an "A" or a lower grade?
- Who are your organization's primary constituencies and the stakeholders on whose support your organization depends? What are the criteria by which they would assess your organization an "A" or lower grade?
This step proves particularly important because understanding what matters to those who have a stake in your organization's success and those you need to enlist in supporting your organization can inspire new strategies for achieving your organization's purpose.

- What is your organization's position in the marketplace?
  - What is your organization's percentage of market share?
  - Who are your organization's primary competitors?
  - What do these organizations do better in attracting and/or serving clients or customers?
  - How do your best competitors approach your clients and what can you learn from that?

Step 4: Looking forward

- What threats are ahead?
- What are the opportunities?
- What does your organization have to continue to do well?
- In what areas does your organization have to do better (to improve, to change, to address, to do more of, do less of, to start, to stop) to be even more effective and successful?

Step 5: Based on your and your group's answers to the above questions, what goals do you want to achieve?

- What are your short-term (3- to 12-month) goals?
- What are your long-term (two- to five-year) goals?
- Of all these goals, what are your top one to seven priorities?

Criteria for Successful Goals

Successful goals share these criteria; they are:

- Clear, specific, and measurable so that they are not susceptible to misinterpretation. This means you need to avoid vague words such as "soon" or "high standards";
- Relevant to your business's bottom line or your organization's purpose;
- Challenging yet attainable (you want your employees to stretch and create breakthroughs; you do not want goals set so high that you frustrate your employees when they never reach them);
- Outcome-based (versus activity-based; it does not matter how many meetings a manager holds if the meetings produce nothing; it is not the number of customers an employee calls on, it is the dollar amounts of the sales that result from those calls that matter).

Scorekeeping

On a personal level, do you step on the scale in the morning, or track on a smartphone the treadmill miles you run or the amount of weights you lift? If so, you realize that even when you are not winning, you like to learn how well you have done. As proof, ask a player or coach about a game just played and he will tell you the score and the game's best plays. Meet with the executive director of a successful nonprofit organization that holds annual strategic planning sessions, and she will tell you the amount of progress her organization has made against measurable milestones.

Scores provide your employees and organization a clear metric for tracking your progress toward goals. In accountable workplaces, employees keep score as they move forward toward their goals; in nonaccountable workplaces, employees do not know the score.

Employees can keep score in areas such as the number of customers seen during the week, the amount of revenue billed per month, the number of compliments given on customer feedback cards, or the decrease in costs or expenses.

Designing a Scorekeeping System

When designing effective scorekeeping measures and methods, keep the following in mind:

- Employees need to be able to self-audit their scores so that they know when they have won.
- Create a system that allows scores to be frequently assessed, creating multiple wins and continued employee excitement.
- Create objective rather than subjective metrics for unambiguous wins.
- Create visible metrics; employees respond best to scores they and others can see.
- Aim for simple, easily understandable and obtainable rather than complex metrics and measures.

Here is how to incorporate scorekeeping and wins into daily work life
A national bank contacted me because their tellers' high turnover resulted in escalating recruiting, onboarding, and training expenses.

I visited three bank branches and asked each teller group, "How do you know when you've done a good job?" Each group of tellers initially remained silent. A few tellers shrugged their shoulders. After two long minutes, one teller in the first group said, "fewer complaints." When another said, "balancing the till faster at the end of the day," a third added, "but if it's not accurate you have to start all over again and if the supervisor sees, you get in trouble."

This experience repeated in all three branches. The tellers' silence and lackluster enthusiasm told me they did not feel they could win. To fix this, the tellers, their supervisors, and I devised simple measures tellers could use for recording "wins" during their entire shift. These included compliments received on "reward for candid feedback cards" given to customers, and contests for fast, accurate end of shift till balancing. Morale shot up and turnover decreased.

What scorekeeping methods can you incorporate into your employees' jobs, allowing them and your organization to win? You can set goals in areas such as the dollar value of sales, percentage increase in market share, dollar value of cross-sales, decreased overhead costs per dollar of sales, number of closes per customer contacted, 4.5 or high scores on a 0 to 5 customer satisfaction scale, or other specific measures unique to your industry.

Scores and Wins Prove Especially Valuable With "Drudge" Tasks

You provide increased motivation for employees who competently handle routine tasks by devising ways in which they can score wins.

One of my grocery store clients engaged their baggers with fastest, secure bagging contests, ultimately winning front-page news stories announcing their winning baggers. Morale in that grocery chain soared.

One restaurant and bar for which I provided mystery shopping services instituted a "cleanest, fastest bussed table" award for their bar on busy Friday and Saturday nights. The wait staff loved it, and the restaurant reaped the rewards of seating more customers on busy weekend evenings, "best of the city awards," exceptionally low wait staff turnover, and record profits.

Focusing Your Coaching on Accountability

The goals you have set and the scorekeeping system you have established enable you to have targeted, productive accountability discussions with each employee. These discussions provide your employees with recognition and guidance, creating alignment in goals and roles from the top to the bottom of your organization.

You can give immediate positive recognition to employees as they achieve goals. You can also share their accomplishments publicly to provide them with peer recognition and to encourage others. If you see an employee's scores decreasing, you can check in privately, and say, "I noticed your success rates going down. What are your thoughts about what's happening?"

Your discussion can include open-ended questions such as:

- What support or resources do you need to better meet your goals and improve your scores?
- As you review your own progress, what is becoming clear to you?

Rewards

Once you have defined goals for your employees and arrived at how you and they will score themselves and monitor their progress, you can decide how to celebrate and reward your employees' achievements.

Will you give bonuses or pay increases? Will you congratulate your employees or ensure that they are recognized for their success? Will you grant your best employees increased autonomy, responsibility, or status? These are the employees who mentor other employees and advocate for your organization with clients and customers. They set a standard that motivates others to similarly excel.

When you reward what you want to see, you increase your employees' commitment to continued excellence. Your reward and recognition system functions best when it celebrates and rewards employees who consistently deliver results.

Figure 5.1 provides you with six incentive categories, four of which can be provided without cost.

Recognition:
- Awards; peer-to-peer applause, and thank you messages; public acknowledgments; certificates of accomplishment; positive feedback; letters of appreciation, publicity in the employer's newsletter; being selected to represent the work unit at meetings

Job Redesign and Cross-Training:
- Assigning new duties; re-designing the current job; making changes in the ratio of preferred duties; giving frequent changes of duties; assigning of preferred work partners; approving of job-related requests; giving rapid follow-up by the manager on job-related issues; giving opportunities for advanced training

Job Responsibilities:
- Opportunity for increased self-management; more power to decide and/or implement changes; more frequent participation in decision-making; more frequent requests to provide input for decisions and recommendations; giving greater opportunity to select one's own goals, priorities or tasks; greater opportunity to schedule time; greater access to information

Tangible Rewards:
- Cash bonuses; restaurant or bookstore gift certificates; commissions; profit sharing; merit increases; lunches on the company; company stock; company donation to charities or a college fund in the employee's name; increased fringe benefits; paid trips to professional meetings or training seminars

Status Indicators:
- Larger work area; computer upgrades; improved equipment; larger windows; a promotion; a more private office; the opportunity to supervise more (or fewer) employees; status symbols (windows, carpeting, nameplate, plants, a key to the executive lounge); invitations to "high-level" meetings; a new title; being placed in a special category (or tenure); the chance to train others

Incentive Feedback:
- Celebrating wins; receiving knowledge of the effect of one's own performance; being informed of eventual results of output; receiving "fan mail"/customer compliments

Figure 5.1 Rewards and incentives

CHAPTER 6

Inspiring Your Employees to Work as One Team

When you transform a group of highly accountable employees into a highly accountable, high-producing team, you supercharge your organization. In the company I ran, our employees melded into a workplace SWAT team, so well-oiled that when any of us needed to be off-site, other team members moved to fill the gap. This chapter teaches you how to create a high-functioning team.

You will learn how to inspire your employees to work harder *and* as one team, united toward a common goal. You will learn nine steps that build a high-performance team and gain an array of tools and strategies for leading high-energy team events.

Team Defined

In a workplace team, employees work collaboratively to achieve their organization's mission and goals. Employees realize they, their coworkers, and managers have complementary roles and skills and share a common purpose. Employee team members commit to mutual accountability, knowing they can achieve more synergistically together than they could independently. Although each employee plays his or her own position, they coordinate with and support one another.

How You Know You Have a Great Team

In a great team, each team member commits to their role and the team's purpose, taking full accountability for the team's results as well as for their individual efforts. Team members know they can count on each other to "hold up their end" and play their role.

Team members share resources and information, producing the synergy of two plus two equals five, instead of four. Communication flows, differences surface, and conflict resolves. The team identifies and tackles problems, threats, and opportunities.

How a Sense of Team Benefits an Organization

Team synergy pays dividends, as a team of employees can accomplish tasks that could not be achieved by individuals working independently. Employees realize how their job fits into the overall effort, orienting them to supporting and coordinating with one another, thus creating a goal alignment among departments and a smoother functioning organization.

Because team members bring diverse skills and talents to bear on complex tasks, the organization reaps benefits in improved decisions, services, and products. Team members do not want to let each other down, with peer pressure inspiring team members to correct any potentially problematic habits and to give their all. The result you and your organization receive will be improved performance and productivity.

A sense of team also reduces turnover. Recent studies document that when employees become embedded in their jobs, they develop a web of connections and relationships that they hesitate to leave.[1]

Employees Benefit From Team

Employees enjoy the feeling of personal and professional support that being a team member gives, leading to increased job satisfaction and morale. Team members transfer insights, skills, and enthusiasm to each other. These increased psychological benefits lead directly to increased team member retention.

What Happens in Organizations That Lack a Sense of Team?

Organizations lacking a sense of team often consist of departmental silos or work groups that create problems for other work groups. Each silo

---

[1] https://shrm.org/hr-today/trends-and-forecasting/special-reports-and-expert-views/Documents/Retaining-Talent.pdf

develops its unique culture, with the buzzwords, needs, and priorities of each silo not easily understood or accepted by members of other silos.

Each work group's focus on its own needs and priorities can result in unresolved problems for other work groups. In a construction company, "field" employees do not understand why the accounting department needs their paperwork completed "by 5," when field workers cannot afford to set aside the "real" work that "pays all of our salaries," and "payroll is automatic, isn't it?" Frontline order takers fail to record crucial details, leaving those processing invoices spending hours backtracking to unravel messes. Service department employees want to wring the necks of sales team members who promise what cannot be done. The organization fails to function like a smoothly oiled machine, frustrating everyone involved.

Turf wars occasionally result, with employees dividing into camps and taking sides, siphoning off energy that could have been directed toward attaining organization goals. Duplication of work by departments that fail to communicate with other departments wastes payroll dollars. Employees forget they are part of one organization and criticize other departments to customers.

When the owner of a small construction company with revenues of $25M called me, he asked, "What exactly do you do? My friend runs a thriving multi-state architectural firm and said I need you." I answered that I made companies more productive, asked him a dozen questions, and said, "I'd like to work with everyone in your company for an hour to ninety minutes. We'll make sure each employee and work group understands what the other employees and work groups need from them."

At first, he did not understand and asked, "You mean my lead guys?"

"I mean everyone."

"What are we going to do again?"

I explained, and he said his guys were construction hands who would not sit for a lecture. I said, "I won't be the one talking, they will."

When I started the meeting, I explained that in any team sport, we count on our team members to step up to the plate and know the positions they play. During the meeting, each work group presented information to the others concerning their priorities and what they needed from the other work groups to do their best work. When one of the carpenters said, "Now it makes sense why you get so upset about the timecards," the payroll team raised their fists in the air in celebration.

Three months later, the owner called and asked, "that worked, can you come back for another session?"

"Is field getting their timecards in on time?"

"Yes."

The construction company continued to improve their teamwork and communications, and grew from $25M to $150M in revenue.

Five Steps to Building a High-Performing, High-Accountable Team

Step Zero

You have already created the foundation to building a high-performing team: hiring well. You have chosen accountable employees who demonstrate work ethic, initiative, excellent communication, interpersonal, and problem-resolving skills. You have onboarded your employees, giving them a solid understanding of your organization's purpose.

The famous "team development wheel" developed in 1965 by researcher Bruce Tuckman and modified by multiple management practitioners defines four stages to team development: forming, storming, norming, and performing.[2]

The following steps provide you actionable strategies enabling you to manage these four stages and exciting team-building exercises that speed you and your team through to the final stage, "performing."

Step 1

Step 1 involves melding individuals into a team by building the bonds between individual team members. In Tuckman's stage one, "forming," team members eye each other politely and feel uncertain about each other's roles on the team. While some team members eagerly interact, others remain watchful and guarded, keeping their thoughts under the surface.

---

[2] https://tandfonline.com/doi/abs/10.1080/13678861003589099

Verbal team members tend to dominate, and others look outside the team to their manager for guidance. At this stage, team members can also jockey for power or position. The leader's job: create the team.

Step 1: Exercises and Tools

As the team's leader, you speed your team through stage one by helping team members form individual and team bonds. Three exercises, "talent bank," "scavenger hunt," and "toxic popcorn," help team members establish these bonds. Teams can also participate in both talent bank and scavenger hunt from remote locations.

Toxic popcorn additionally surprises team members concerning their fellow team members' creative problem-solving and collaborative skills, as some team members initially consider the task impossible and then find other members inspirationally wading-in with creative solutions. Individuals work closely with others they have not earlier worked with and develop camaraderie. Toxic popcorn also bonds a team through their shared victory as they accomplish a challenging task.

Talent Bank

For a team to play with full engagement, team members need to learn more of each other's personalities background and skills. In "talent bank," each team member provides short answers to three questions:

1. "What are two talents I bring to the team?"
2. "What led me/leads me to commit to this organization?"
3. "What is a goal I have?"

After each team member has spoken, the team leader asks, "What are your thoughts based on what you've learned concerning what your fellow team members bring to the team?" Common answers include:

- "I found out so many things I didn't know."
- "I have a lot more in common with some of the team mates than I knew."

- "I'm excited by the goals I've heard."
- "I feel much closer to my teammates."
- "What an impressive team; we can accomplish anything!"

Other questions you can ask as the team leader include:

- "What common goals did you hear?"
- "What was your biggest surprise?"

Scavenger Hunt

"Scavenger hunt" provides a light-hearted team activity that introduces team members to each other. Prior to the activity, a staff member collects important and interesting facts about each team member and puts them into scavenger hunt questions, such as "which team member speaks five languages," "which team member was a Green Beret," or "which team member rappels from cliffs on the weekends?"

Each team member then receives a list of 12 fact-based statements and "wins" the hunt when s/he successfully finds a team member who fits each fact. Team member scavenger searching can be accomplished in-person, via texting or instant messenger or chat room interactions.

Teams find this "talent/background" scavenger hunt exciting. Common answers to "what do you think about this exercise" include:

"It was exciting."

"I love what I found about my teammates."

"I guess I can't hide my light under bushel basket anymore" (voiced by one of the team's quieter members).

"I now know better who to call on when I need help on a couple projects I'm tackling."

Toxic Popcorn

"Toxic popcorn" both unites a team and reveals a team's strengths and weaknesses and can most successfully be played by teams of five to seven members. Teams love playing "toxic popcorn" and describe the experience as fun, exciting, valuable, and bonding.

When your team totals more than seven, you can ask one or two additional team members to take on the role of observers (and to enter into team play if the team has a "spill") or you can run several concurrent toxic popcorn circles.

At the start, you lay a large rope circle of 10 feet in diameter on the ground. At the circle's center, place two large tin cans of the type that hold 34.5 ounces of coffee, with dimensions of six inches in diameter and six to seven inches in height. Figure 6.1 shows you toxic popcorn's initial configuration.

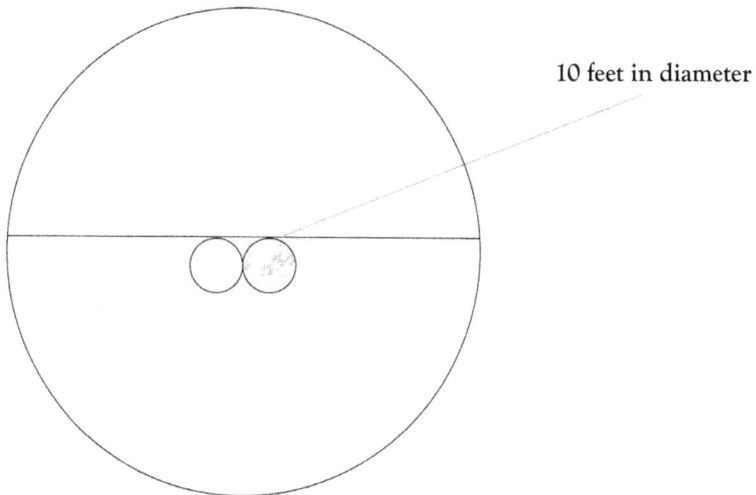

10 feet in diameter

Figure 6.1 Toxic popcorn circle

Hand each team an uninflated bicycle inner tube and each team member a piece of rope one-quarter to one-half centimeter in width and seven feet in length. Into one can, you place two cups of popcorn kernels.

You then tell the team:

Your challenge: A can of toxic popcorn has the potential to contaminate a larger area; however, a rope circle currently contains the contamination. The toxic area extends to the ceiling; the rope may not be touched or moved. If the poisonous popcorn is not transferred to a safe container for decontamination, the toxic popcorn may explode. Estimates suggest the popcorn has a safe life of 30 minutes before explosion.

One of the two cans inside the circle contains toxic popcorn. The safe container is available for decontamination. Your team succeeds if it can find a way to safely transfer the toxic popcorn from the can holding the kernels to the safe container, using only the materials provided to you (the seven-feet rope and the bicycle tire tube).

You then give the team rules. These include:

1. Each team member must remain outside the circle and not cross the plane of the circle with any part of his or her body. If this occurs, they step to the side and do not participate in any form. Another observer team member may replace the departing team member. Alternatively, you may invite the departing team members to return after two minutes.
2. The group is responsible for the safety of all team members. No member may sacrifice another team member or him/herself to aid in the transfer of the kernels.
3. The rope circle needs to stay in place, and not be kicked or moved.
4. No spills are allowed.
5. Team members may only use the materials provided; however, they may be used in any manner desired, other than cutting the bicycle tube.
6. Team members have no protection inside the cylinder created by the 10 feet in diameter circle. The kernels will not spread their toxicity to the ropes, the bicycle inner tube, the safe can, or the instruction giver.
7. The can holding the kernels needs to stay inside the circle and remain within one foot of the center. The other can may move anywhere inside or outside the circle.
8. Your team needs to transfer all kernels into the safe can within 30 minutes.

Toxic Popcorn Discussion Questions

After the team safely completes its mission (a leader's guide to how a team can safety complete this challenge is provided at the end of this section), ask them to debrief themselves, using the following questions. You can then provide them your feedback.

1. Did your team have a team leader, and who was it? What did s/he do to lead? Was there more than one leader? How did it happen that the leaders became the leaders?
2. How effective was your team in accomplishing its task (with no spill)?
3. How effective was your team in working together as a team? What helped your team to succeed?
4. What did individual team members do that helped the team succeed?
5. What got in the way of your team accomplishing its task?
6. What got in the way of your team working together effectively?
7. How did your participation in this exercise reflect how you usually operate/behave? If you acted the way you normally act, what did you learn? If you acted differently than normal, what did you learn from that?
8. What did you learn, relearn, or gain from the activity (about team-work, about not giving up, about creative problem-resolving, about listening)?
9. What of the preceding learning can you apply to your work?

What You May Learn About Your Team by Using Toxic Popcorn

Teams reveal their strengths and weaknesses when playing toxic popcorn. Real-life examples that you can then use to coach your team include:

- Some individuals who initially view the task as impossible marvel at how their team succeeds and later state "we can do anything."
- Teams rush to transfer the popcorn, spilling it (if this occurs, you can call "do over" and give them another chance).
- Two dominant members argue over transfer methods and, in their excitement, one or both forget to listen; often, this results in a team member shutting down or shouting.
- Teams subdivide into camps, each often led by a leader, and need to negotiate methods with one another.

- Verbally dominant team members ignore one or more individuals who speak softly, missing ideas that would have helped the team succeed more quickly.
- A thoughtful team member becomes a leader and gains his or her team's long-lasting respect.
- Team members laugh with each other and celebrate victory once they successfully complete their task.
- Some teams forget to use all their resources, in particular the uninflated bicycle inner tube, and as a result, spill during the transfer.
- Some teams practice, developing multiple strategies, and demonstrating flexibility and adaptability as they test out their methods.
- Lone rangers find the toxic popcorn activity intriguing, and in the process, integrate into the team.

Solving the Toxic Popcorn Challenge

Although teams can successfully transfer the popcorn kernels from one container to the other using only ropes, the easiest method involves using the uninflated bicycle inner tube. (If a team does not use the tube, you can comment on this fact during your debriefing.)

Teams can effectively complete the transfer by tightening the tube, tying it with ropes, lassoing one can, and raising it to tilt the kernels into another can. The most successful teams gather, discuss the challenge, and practice using the empty can. Ordinarily, it takes every team member's hands on the ropes to provide the needed tension to lift and pour the popcorn kernels from one can to another.

Step 2: Dealing With "Storming" and Developing Team Alignment

In team development stage two, "storming," team members have grown more confident about their team's overall strengths. At the same time, some team members may remain uncertain about one or more teammates. Still, other team members, concerned about hierarchy, may compete for status, position in the corporate hierarchy, or recognition from other team members or other members of management.

The initial enjoyment of being on a team and the need to be polite have worn off, and members begin to "test" each other. When the team takes on hard challenges and needs to meld varying skill sets and individuals with different operating styles, disagreements on approach can erupt. Personalities may clash. Some members could grow frustrated with those they feel do not pull their weight.

Emotions sometimes run high. Some team members give "we're a team" lip service, but opt out and default to solo action when teamwork becomes too difficult.

The differences in natural working styles that often result in conflict include:

- Random (there are many potential routes to take) versus sequential (there is a best route, and we need to take the steps in order)
- Abstract (let us establish the big picture, and the day to day will fall into place) versus concrete (the devil is in the details)
- Intuitive (I listen to my instincts) versus sensory (I pay attention to what I see)
- Closure (we need to come to a decision) versus open-ended (let us not end the discussion too quickly)
- Logical (what makes sense) versus feeling (how will this impact others and ourselves)

Step 2: Exercises and Tools

You can use three engaging, inspiring exercises to help your team move through stage two quickly. "Helium" and "balloons" show team members how valuable being on a team can be, and often force team members to confront that they allow their individual focus and competition to impede their ability to fully engage on a team. "Pie" takes a team to the next level. When I work with organizations for multiple years in a row, the organization's leaders always ask that we again conduct "pie."

Helium

"Helium" surprises team members with a task that seems simple yet proves to be highly challenging. Each team of four to eight individuals holds a 3/8-inch wooden dowel measuring five feet in length.

Team members line up on both sides of the dowel, and each member holds out their two horizontal index fingers. Their job—work as a team to lower the dowel to the floor, while abiding by a few simple rules. The rules: each team member needs to keep two index fingers in contact with the dowel at all times; the team members need to hold their fingers straight and horizontal, and the dowel needs to remain level.

Here is what happens—even though the team concentrates on lowering the dowel, it rises. Why? Team members focus so hard on their fingers (their task) that they lose a team focus. The team only accomplishes their job when the team works as one, aligned team.

Balloons

"Balloons" makes it clear how an entire company of employees wins.

Here is how to run this exercise. Divide your employee group into teams (of three to eight employees), and then give each team a roll of masking tape and bag of 25 or more birthday party-sized balloons to blow up.

Let employees know that the name of the game is "balloons" and **"the way to win is to build the tallest possible free-standing balloon tower they can,"** using the maximum number of balloons. Employees spring into action, charmed by the chance to play with balloons at work. Each team works like clockwork, blowing up and taping balloons and discussing how to build the tallest, free-standing tower they possibly can.

Remind employees every few minutes that the way to win is to build the tallest possible free-standing balloon tower they can, using the maximum number of balloons. Employees continue to work, ignoring you or wondering why you keep repeating that phrase. Occasionally, someone accidentally pops a balloon and members in other teams may cheer. Occasionally, employees from one team attempt to steal balloons from another team.

Eventually, one employee keys on the "maximum number of balloons" phrase and realizes that all the teams need to combine with all of the other teams' balloon towers to win. When the employees realize this, they move together with excitement and create a huge balloon tower.

After that, you as their leader can pull them into a discussion about how all the departments and teams working together have a more successful outcome than when they focus solely on their individual department or team efforts. The balloon tower serves as a colorful metaphor and reminder.

The managers of one large, Seattle-based global freight company left the resulting balloon tower in the company lunchroom for weeks, ultimately making and laminating a large poster of the tower, reminding all employees that warehouse, shipping, receiving, accounting, sales, service, and administrative staff need to work together.

Pie

On winning teams, each member understands what other team members and work groups are doing and why, so all team members can effectively communicate, coordinate, collaborate, and support each other. This understanding proves invaluable to all teams and organizations.

"Pie" begins with each team member or work unit outlining their main goals and priorities to other team members or work units.

Next, each team member or work group explains how and why they depend on other team members or work groups for support to accomplish their missions. This section of the activity builds a concrete sense of interconnectedness and mutual dependency.

Third, using the "pie" as a metaphor, each team member or work group outlines what their slice of the pie is. The metaphor allows the group to creatively explain how they view themselves within the larger whole.

Do they or does their group represent one slice, or do they consider themselves the largest slice? In one hospital, the nurses suggested that their slice amounted to 75 percent of the pie. The physicians looked on in shock.

Or, are they the filling, the pan, the cherry on top, the chef, or the oven that bakes the pie? In one contentious organization, seven work groups defined their role as chef. In another very messy organization, all but two groups described themselves as the pie's filling.

Some groups describe themselves as the crust, either due to their personality or how they provide cover to other groups. One group described itself as a tartlet that sat to the side of the pie, because they did not feel connected. Another group explained that they considered themselves cornstarch, as none of the other teams seemed to realize they existed.

For a team to play with full engagement, team members need to know where each member is coming from. The final step of "pie" asks that each member or work group tell the others "here's what I wish my team members and the work groups with whom we work would understand."

Four Real-Life Examples Showing How "Pie" Improves Team/ Organizational Productivity

The "pie" exercise's last question gives team members and teams the opportunity to safely put on the table what needs to be said and understood to increase organizational productivity.

Newspaper: What Your Department Does Costs Us Hours

Years ago, the publisher of Anchorage's underdog newspaper asked me if I could help their paper overcome the larger newspaper's market share by the end of the year. I asked him for an hour with his managers.

We focused the meeting on the "what I wish the other managers understood" topic. The head of circulation said he wished the newsroom would understand that their 'just another minute' request to the print room costs us 12 hours." He explained, "Everything here runs on a painfully tight time frame. If the newsroom holds the presses for an extra minute because they want to perfect a headline or load final game scores, thousands of papers arrive on the loading dock a crucial minute late. The carriers' contract allows them to leave if the papers aren't ready by the deadline. That means the circulation department spends the next twelve hours delivering papers and fielding customer calls complaining because their papers arrived late."

Hospital: The Emperor Has No Clothes

This question allows employees to safely say, "the Emperor has no clothes" to senior managers. The head of housekeeping at a midsized hospital surprised the hospital's chief executive officer (CEO) when she said that she considered his wastebasket her desktop.

When he asked, "What does that mean?" she explained that he told her weekly to keep overtime down and she considered infection, patient rooms, and common area cleanliness her small staff's priorities. "After thirteen-hour days when I'm heading home for the night, I sweep through the administrative offices. If I see a few papers in your wastebasket, I leave them for the next day in the same way that you leave papers on your desk to be tackled the next day. But I always get an e-mail asking, 'Did you forget our wastebaskets?'"

The housekeeping manager's good humor when she delivered her explanation softened her message even as she brought it home.

Distributorship: You Think We Are Not as Important As You Are

Frequent complaints between sales, warehouse, and delivery plagued a large liquor distributorship. During the "I wish you understood" segment, the leader of the drivers' team stood up and said, "You think we're *just* drivers. Have you ever thought about how much intelligence it takes to quickly navigate to delivery sites given rapidly changing traffic conditions and weather?"

"When we arrive at liquor stores, we're the face of this company. They expect us to know what certain wines taste like. At personal expense, many of us buy a lot of our product so we can answer customer questions."

"Here's what happens when you say, 'customer X needs this delivered right away.' If we've already fully loaded the truck, and that customer's product is at the rear, we have to unload and reload the entire truck to accomplish what you asked. As a result, every other customer's orders get delayed—and then you blame us." After the driver leader sat down, the other attendees stood and clapped for him.

Global Supply Chain Company/Acquisition and Merger: We Have Not Yet Become One

Several years after a large, multistate global supply chain company acquired several smaller companies, the senior managers called and said, "We're still operating like separate companies. What can we do, or can you do for us?" We brought the leadership together with the managers and supervisors from each of the former companies together. We started with talent bank, toxic popcorn, helium, and then moved into "pie."

In between the team exercises, I led group discussions concerning what was working well and what needed to change so that the company as whole could improve. After we had completed all four exercises and the group discussions, manager after manager said, "We became one company today. We now know each other's priorities. We put truth on the table."

Step 3: Establishing the Team's Direction and "Norms"

In step 3, the leader assists the employee team or teams in establishing operational agreements so that they can fully leverage their collective efforts and function independently of the leader in achieving organizational goals. This step coincides with the team development wheel's stage three, "norming." During this stage, team members engage openly with each other, confront issues, develop increased cohesion, and work together with increased effectiveness.

Step 3: Exercises and Tools

"Team metaphor" provides teams with collective insight into their team's functioning and helps them envision how they could function more successfully. "Step to the plate" clarifies the effort team members expect from each other. "Rules of engagement" allow teams to successfully navigate touchy problems as a team, so the leader need not step in.

Team Metaphor

Team metaphor offers team members a chance to describe how their team presently operates and how they would like the team to operate. Team members, working in small groups, provide a metaphor for how the team now operates. For example, does their present team resemble:

- A relay team, with runners passing the baton
- A U.S. Olympic ski team, in which everyone functions as a soloist
- A softball team, in which everyone comes up to bat, but handles a unique position in the outfield
- A roller derby team where members elbow each other as they speed around
- A high-school band
- Or, another team

Next, they discuss the metaphor that describes the type of team they want to become. Sample options include:

- The Harlem Globetrotters
- A world-class orchestra
- A SWAT team
- An award-winning dog sled team in which all involved clearly know who is the musher and who is the lead dog
- An operating room team than handles open-heart surgery
- A smoothly functioning entrepreneurial team that builds and markets a new product and quickly takes a lead position in the marketplace
- Or another example of an inspirational team

After each team reports their thoughts, the full group selects their favorite metaphor. Then, they work as a team to strategize what they need to do to become that type of team.

"Step to the Plate"

Hidden, unfulfilled expectations can throttle teams and create energy-sapping conflict, while stated expectations inspire team alignment. When each team member puts on the table what they expect out of their fellow team members and receives voiced commitment and later visible adherence to those expectations, it boosts team member satisfaction and collective productivity.

During an expectations exchange, each team member outlines their expectations of each other and the full team discusses and reaches consensus on the expectations to which all commit.

Here are sample team expectations that you might offer to get your team started on this exercise:

- Speak honestly and communicate frequently, clearly, and directly
- Arrive on time for meetings
- Respond to e-mails within 24 hours
- Listen nondefensively to improvement-oriented comments
- If you have an issue with another member, raise it directly and privately to the person you have the issue with
- Focus on solutions and not blame
- Assume others have positive intentions
- Consider yourself personally responsible for the team's progress, productivity, and success

Rules of Engagement Discussions

Rules of engagement discussions enable the team to negotiate their way through touchy issues that could derail them. This real-life story offers a dramatic example for how a leader can use rules of engagement to improve the functioning of a team with problematic underlying issues.

When the CEO of an international professional services firm asked me to facilitate a day-and-a-half meeting with his 12 junior partners, he did not tell me that he and his partners had told the last facilitator of a planned two-day event to go home after two hours. Instead, he said,

"I have folks coming from four locations and anticipate an easy event. Here's the agenda we'd like you to facilitate. Everyone's already seen it."

When the twelve attendees arrived, I noticed how stiffly they greeted each other. After I handed out the agenda I'd received, two individuals stood and said, "It is a fine agenda but it doesn't address the most important issues. We are not sure we want to be part of this organization." The CEO and his senior managers looked shocked, and I sensed that if I did not respond quickly, these two would leave.

"We definitely have a lot to discuss then," I quickly said. "Let me outline meeting rules of engagement and then we'll discuss the topics you two want to add to the agenda."

Everyone sat. I swiftly wrote the following rules of engagement on the whiteboard, knowing from experience that using them would keep the discussion on course to a positive conclusion. These rules include:

1. Please say nothing you will regret.
2. Please say what is important. By speaking honestly and diplomatically about the issues, you increase our team's chance of attaining true success. When real issues remain unsaid to those who most need to hear them, they cannot be addressed.
3. How you word something is important; for example, "When I see your face, time stands still" versus "You have a face that would stop a clock."
4. Listen. To really listen, it is important that you remain open as you hear others' perspectives. If your framework is "why won't they hear me first," then this session will not work as effectively as it could. Even when you do not like what you hear, it is better if you hear it.
5. Please ask a question if another person says something you will not understand or disagree with. Ask questions that start with "what" or "how," and not "why" or "did."
6. Feedback: when you are giving feedback, please exercise self-control in how you say what you need to say. Give your comments so that the other person gets their meaning without feeling attacked. Figure 6.2 shows diagrammatically how to do this. In this figure, the center line represents today's date. If you seek changes, define them as the future improvements or results you hope to see, instead of the past problem, so that the other person does not feel personally blamed.

PROBLEM   VS.   **EXPECTATION**

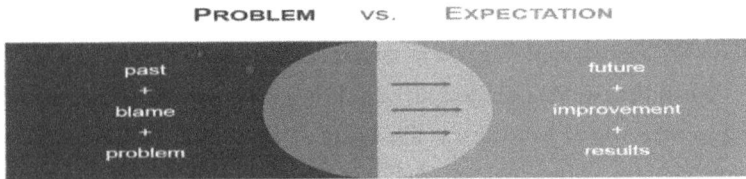

Figure 6.2 Problem versus expectation

7. Please focus on "land" not "religion." This guideline, borrowed from former secretary of state Henry Kissinger, refers to his statements that in the Middle East, residents may ultimately be able to agree on land even if they cannot agree on religion. In an organization, we do not always agree with each other's personalities, but we can agree on how we communicate and interact.

8. Please handle criticism professionally: ask a question so you understand the criticism, instead of shutting down, becoming defensive, or attacking back.

9. "75" watts: using the light bulb as a metaphor, if your voice raises to 100 hundred watts, I will ask you to tone it down to 75 watts, so the next person does not escalate to 150 watts.

10. Please be concise.

11. Please demonstrate respect.

Once I outlined the rules of engagement, and with the CEO's permission, I asked the two individuals who had stood what they wanted added to the agenda. They stated that they were considering leaving the company and had received offers from a competing firm. I asked the other partners what they wanted added as well. It turned out that everyone, other than the CEO and one of his long-term associates, had grown highly dissatisfied with other partners and how the firm was centrally managed.

The discussions lasted beyond 7 p.m. that evening and then continued all day Sunday, despite, as several partners said, "I can't believe we're ruining Super Bowl Sunday. But I'm glad we're doing this."

By Sunday evening, the discussions concerning what partners expected of each other and the managing partner; how conflict and decision making needed to be handled; how workload was allocated; and other hot issues gave birth to a new organization, one with a new name and complete buy-in from all partners.

Step 4: Your Highly Accountable Team Performs Miracles

Step 4 coincides with the team development wheel's fourth and final stage, "performing." Teams that reach stage four focus on getting the job done, using resources efficiently, and driving full speed ahead toward the goal, fully committed to winning for their employer. Characteristics of a team that has reached stage five include:

- Open and supportive communication between and among team members and management
- Ownership
- Synergy, such that two plus two equals five
- Agile and flexible
- Confident and motivated
- "On the same page"
- Able to operate without supervision

Step 4: Tool/Exercise Operating Agreement Creation

When a team transitions into stage four, it strengthens its continuing success by drafting operating agreements. These customized rules of engagement, crafted by the team, define in writing the standards the team intends to live by.

Three Type A managers drafted the following sample operating agreements when they had to transition quickly from "storming" to "performing." Like bellicose bulls, these three senior managers were used to knocking heads against each other for weekly one-hour meetings in the presence of their strong CEO. They respected him and listened when, after hearing their quarrels, he defined a path forward each week.

When the CEO wound up in the hospital with a triple bypass, he called and asked me, "Can you transform my three thick-headed senior leaders into a team so I don't have to mediate disputes from my hospital bed? I've told them to expect you. They're right now deciding how they plan to run things in my absence."

I said, "Sure," and headed over to their corporate offices at noon. When I got there, the Type A's shoed me away. "We've got it all worked out."

"Really?"

"Yes, we'll meet for an hour every morning and have the same discussions we used to have in the weekly meeting."

"What happens when one of the three of you needs to travel or be on-site handling an emergency?"

"He'll have to connect in."

"So, five hours of meetings every week?"

"We're anticipating longer than an hour, especially in the beginning."

"How long were you at it this morning?"

"We just finished."

"You started—"

"At 7," he said impatiently.

"So, five hours this morning and you're planning to meet a minimum of five days a week for at least an hour each day. How do you plan to shoehorn these meetings into your already heavy workloads?"

They looked irritated, and I said, "Let me save you some time." The actual operating agreements they crafted (provided below) included: "The three of us will become a real team. Each of the three of us will understand each other's thinking process and the parameters important to each other. Because of that, any one of us will be able to make decisions that the other two will feel comfortable with."

Figure 6.2 Sample operating agreements

We have agreed to:

- Meet at 7:15 every morning for 30 minutes; during this meeting, we will resolve daily crises and deal with hot issues.
- Once a week, we will hold a meeting of approximately one hour to work through substantial issues that need in-depth discussions.

We have agreed that when discussing issues:

- We will not talk over each other.

- We will fully debate significant decisions and use collaborative negotiation.
- We will individually fully commit to and support team decisions.
- We will make decisions that are in the best interests of our company.
- We will be careful not to half-heartedly compromise because the decision-making process is taking too long and we are "worn down."

We have agreed that when there is conflict, we will:

- Realize the good intentions of each party.
- Clarify and pinpoint the stumbling block(s).
- Reflect on our individual positions and consider whether they need to be modified.
- Surface all hidden objectives and reservations.
- Resolve any issues between ourselves and not share our conflicts with others.
- Be candid and open with each other and put all of our thoughts "on the table."
- Call in a neutral third-party facilitator if we reach a stalemate.
- Approach major differences of opinion from a process of mutual education concerning the issues and concerns that lead each of us to reach our "positions."

When the CEO checked in with his three managers a week later, he called me and said, "It's going to be a lot easier when I return. My three senior managers now work together. I won't have to step in so often as the mediator and decision-maker. They've also learned from each other and are better managers of their departments."

Step 5: Monitoring and Continuously Improving

Your last step is to regularly assess your team's output and operations so that you can continuously improve it. This step takes you past Tuckman's team development wheel because your team has formed. Now, you want to assess and refine your team's operations.

These nine questions enable you and your team to review your team's output, focus, and operations.

Output:
- What results does our team produce?
- Which positive results are attributable to effective teamwork, and could not as easily been created by team members working separately and individually?

Focus:
- Is our team focusing on the high-priority issues that it needs to in the context of producing results for our organization?
- What topics/tasks should we focus on during our team meetings?
- What issues take up our valuable time that should not?

Leveraging our talent:
- Is each team member's role clear to the other team members?
- How can we better leverage our individual and collective talents?

Methods:
- How are our communication and conflict resolution methods working for us? What improvements do we need to make?
- How is our decision-making process working for us? What improvements do we need to make?

Alternatively, Table 6.1 provides you a team evaluation rating chart you can use to allow team members to quickly rate their team in nine areas.

Table 6.1 Team evaluation rating chart

Team Evaluation Rating Chart	Disagree Strongly	Disagree	Disagree Slightly	Agree Slightly	Agree	Agree Strongly
We have a clear and exciting mission or role/purpose as a team.						
We have challenging team goals with specific targets and steps to guide us toward those goals.						
Each person understands his/her team role, authority for making decisions and taking action, and how he/she must support others on the team						
We have clear procedures for meetings and for working with other teams, to enable our team to remain focused on our goals.						
We have systems for regularly reviewing our performance and identifying actions for improving team results and the contribution of each member.						
We meet only when there's good reason and our discussions and meetings are to the point, involve all team members, and end with clear action plans.						
We have problem solving and decision-making methods that help us generate quality decisions and solutions to which people feel committed.						
Team members communicate openly and effectively, listen to one another's views, and have productive discussions about important issues						
We are skilled at dealing with conflicts among team members before things get disruptive and out of hand.						

CHAPTER 7

Pressing Reset if Employees Start to Slip From Accountability

When employees do not show accountability, things begin to go awry. Employees lacking in accountability miss deadlines, break promises, and do not act on or even realize their ownership. These employees move into passenger seat mode. If you allow this to happen, your organization slips from a culture of accountability into a culture of confusion, conflict avoidance, or abdication.

In Chapter 7, you will learn how to quickly press the reset button should an employee start to slip in accountability. You will gain solid skills and strategies for addressing and resolving the work performance and attitude issues before they get in the way of maximum performance.

This chapter includes an example of a one-question "reset" conversation that realigned an employee who had temporarily lost his/her way. The chapter concludes with a script based on a real-life scenario that outlines an accountability reset discussion that led an employee to make dramatic, positive changes.

Your Leadership Role

As the leader, it falls to you to hold individual employees and your full employee team, as well as yourself, accountable. When you do not, you allow a less-accountable employee to frustrate and burden other employees and to erode morale and your organization's culture. If you hesitate to tackle on an accountability issue or a work performance or attitudinal problem, consider the following:

- Each time a leader accepts undesirable work or behavior, they lower standards for the entire organization, which can disillusion and disenfranchise your managers and accountable employees.

- If a leader/manager puts up with or allows those who lack accountability to remain on the team, they will spend valuable time solving the problems the nonachiever created; time that could instead be spent on strategy or on maximizing the output of high achievers.
- A less-accountable employee pulls down the entire group's total achievement and motivation.
- When a leader accepts the below-standard performance, they burden other employees who carry much of the low-achiever's workload.
- A leader damages their leadership image when they do not act swiftly to resolve problems.

Holding Employees Accountable

Your approach makes all the difference in resetting an employee's accountability. The following guidelines provide an approach that creates positive results.

Partner With Your Employee

Your employee has more control over how much effort they invest in work than you do. As a result, you need to engage and motivate your employee if you want them to be fully accountable. This requires that you get through to the mental space from which your employee makes decisions. You do this best by asking your employee questions because ultimately your employee hears louder what they say in answer to your questions, than what you say to them.

No Time Like the Present

Deal with problematic behavior early before habits become ingrained, or other employees wonder why you let one employee slack off or even replicate the problem behaviors.

An Effective Launch to Your Coaching Discussion

How you begin the reset discussion matters. Start your discussion on a positive note and eliminate the defensive wall or evasive smoke screen your employee may erect or take shelter behind. Surprise your employee with the thought that the discussion will result in a win/win outcome.

Begin by saying, "I'd like us to have a positive and productive discussion. I'll know we've had a great discussion if when we finish it you feel it was great, and I do as well." Alternatively, you might tell your employee you want to bring something to his/her attention so that the two of you can get on the same page.

You can also conduct a reset discussion during a regular weekly check-in with your employee and slide into it after your employee debriefs you concerning how they are doing on their projects. If you select this beginning, you might start your part of the discussion with, "I'd like to raise something so you and I can discuss it together. How frank do you want me to be?" I have used this stage-setting several thousand times when having "acting manager" discussions on behalf of my clients, and invariably the response this question generates is an employee sitting up straight and saying, "I want you to be honest."

In your discussion, make respect your compass and honesty your rudder. By speaking respectfully, honestly, openly, directly, and diplomatically and by listening to what your employee says, you will convince your employee s/he can be equally open and honest. Remember: you seek to convince. Accountability is a choice, not a hammer.

Pave the Way to Success With Two-Way Dialogue

No matter how eloquently you speak, your employee can tune out when you talk but not when they need to answer questions. Aim for a 75 percent (your employee talking) to 25 percent (you speaking) ratio in your discussion.

Use questioning and respectful listening to:

- Uncover what is going on for your employees; there may be a lot happening, both personally and professionally, that you are unaware of.

- Transfer responsibility to your employee's shoulders. Neither you nor your employee succeeds long term when you work harder at improving your employee than they do. You need your employee to choose positive change.

Employ open-ended searching questions such as:

- "Where do you want to be in six to twelve months in your career?"
- "What do you think you need to do to get there?"
- "When do you plan to start?"
- "How will it benefit you to change your habits?"
- "What's getting in your way?"
- "How does what you're doing or not doing impact the team?"
- "How can I, as your coach, better support you?"

Unearth the Sweet Spot

An employee makes genuine, lasting changes for their own personal reasons. Continue your dialogue until you surface what matters to your employee, otherwise known as their "sweet spot." If you have not heard this term before, the sweet spot on a bat or racket is the area that makes most effective contact with a ball, resulting in the maximum response for a given amount of effort.

I learned the incredible impact of "sweet spot" when I informally fostered eight 15- to 18-year-old teenage boys during a three-year period. Some had dropped out of high school. Others had been in and out of jail. Most were on the outs with one or both parents. Several of these young men had children with whom they had no contact.

Every boy continued with ingrained problem behaviors and habits until they discovered their personal "sweet spot" that propelled them to make changes and turn their lives around. One young man dug deep into himself and handled both work and personal frustrations to be able to be a better dad for his child than the father he had grown up with.

Another thrived under the respect he received from a caring adult who saw his potential. He changed his ways to become a person who would continue to receive respect.

One young man connected with an employer who took a chance on him. When he realized his habits risked the job and his chance to make something of himself, he changed his ways.

Still, another decided to go to court to gain custody of his children and knew he did not stand a chance until he showed he gained a General Educational Development (GED) and held down a job with compensation adequate to support his child and himself.

Each of these young men graduated from high school or received GEDs. All found and held down jobs. Those who had children regained full or partial custody of their children. If this success proved possible for problem teenage boys, realize how much easier it can be with the functional men and woman who work for you. Find what matters to each of them and link it to accountability.

How the Sweet Spot Might Work: Turning Around an Employee With One Question

The notes you took during your hiring interview and weekly "check-in" interviews prove invaluable in unearthing your employee's sweet spot. While you may find that your employee's motivations have changed, or that they have a pattern of "starting strong, finishing weak," you can still use your employee's own words to accomplish a reset.

Regarding an employee I will call Van, I used the notes her manager took during his hiring interview to help turn Van around with one note-based question. When her manager initially interviewed "Van," he had asked, "If hired, what do you want to have happen when working for me?"

Van had answered, "I want you to trust and rely on me, to give me increasing amounts of responsibility. I want you to delegate challenging projects to me so I can show what I can do and can grow." Van and her supervisor worked together well for close to a year when Van became unexpectedly pregnant after sleeping with an individual who had said he had a vasectomy.

Overnight, Van changed from a terrific executive assistant into a train wreck. She missed crucial deadlines. She forgot details and some projects altogether. She turned in sloppy work. The manager called me and said, "I don't want to fire her, but she's a disaster. Every day I bring up problems, and she gives me a spaced-out look and says, 'I'll be okay.' But she's not okay. We're in our second week of this."

Van met with me in my client's conference room. I pulled her hiring interview notes and read them to her. "Van, this is what you said you wanted during your initial hiring interview. Your manager wants it for you as well. So, when do you again become the employee he can rely on and trust to give increasing responsibility and challenging projects?"

Van's words seemed to ring in her ears, as if I had dropped them like stones into a well. She sat quiet, hearing the echoes of her prior words and goals, and then said, "Enough said."

Van then walked into her manager's office and said, "I'm back."

Expectation and Outcome-Focused

Focus your discussion on specific outcomes that show your employee the conversation has shifted to an accountability orientation. As discussed in an earlier chapter and using the center line in Figure 7.1 as today's date, outline the improvements and results you hope to see in the future.

The past is already past, and bringing it up can inspire defensiveness and justification.

Word these outcomes specifically, positively, concretely, objectively, and measurably, as in:

- "Complete all assignments by deadline."
- "Adhere to our organization's quality standard in every product you provide customers."

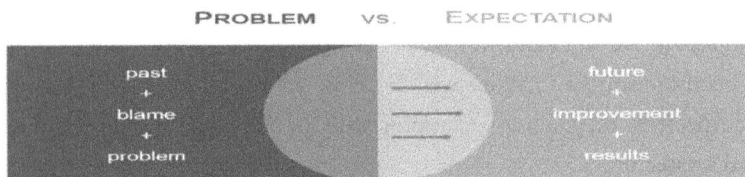

PROBLEM   vs.   EXPECTATION

past		future
+		+
blame		improvement
+		+
problem		results

Figure 7.1 Problem versus expectation

As soon as you bring up the expectation or desired outcome, ask open-ended questions that get your employee talking about his/her views and understanding of the expectations and the reasons why it is important. You want your employee to leave the meeting with a crystal-clear understanding of what they need to do, as well as what achieving the expectation or outcome means to the employee, their team, and the organization.

End your meeting on a positive note and with a set date when you and your employee will meet again to review progress or the successful meeting of the expectations.

Honesty Does Not Need to Sting

You do not need to dance around the truth or mince words when letting your employee know the changes you need to see from him/her, or what consequences may result from lack of improvement. Straightforward honesty produces the best results. If you sense a parental, judgmental tone creeping into your words, however, remember you are the coach and partner, not the judge and jury.

Play Your "A" Game

If your employee rationalizes his/her performance deficiencies, realize that it may take several coaching sessions with redirection, probing questions, and feedback to bring out your employee's inner ownership. Train your ear to hear justifications or excuses as static, while listening for the song underneath that tells you what motivates your employee. If you find yourself reacting, take a calming breath and remember your goal—to either reset this employee's accountability meter or bless him/her out the door.

When you ask tough questions during this meeting, you may find yourself tempted to accept the first answer you receive after asking a question. Those answers, however, may prove to be what your employee thinks you want to hear. Follow-up on the answers your employee gives by asking your employee to "put legs on it" and tell you how s/he specifically plans to accomplish what s/he commits to.

Script

This script provides the play-by-play action for an accountability reset. The employee is a charismatic trainer who knows how to please clients by delivering A+ training sessions. Unfortunately, he recently began to take the easy way through his workload by short-cutting his session preparation time.

As a result, he wows clients with his training session delivery, but clients accustomed to receiving top-notch training session materials accompanying the sessions have let the manager know they feel disappointed. The manager reviews the handout packages for the last two sessions and considers them scanty. He also sees awkward wording describing key concepts—errors that could have been caught by a careful presession review.

For clarity, the employee's words are italicized.

"Jim, thanks for stopping by. How'd today go?"

As the employee gives his answer, the manager listens, and perhaps nods encouragingly or asks additional questions based on what the employee says.

"I want to bring up something and get your thoughts about it."

"Sure."

"I want to find out your thoughts about the value of handouts in training sessions." Note, at this point, the employee knows something is up. He is aware that he is been underperforming in the area of creating quality training session handout packages.

"They're important."

"Good, I'm glad to hear you see that. Jim, you are an incredibly skilled trainer. I'm glad you're on our team. I'd like us to have a positive and productive discussion. My goal is that you and I both feel that it was positive and productive."

"Okay."

"Please tell me about the Lantry session handouts."

"I provided what I thought met the need."

"And the Celdon session handouts?"

"I was pressed for time."

"If you hadn't been pressed for time, what would they have looked like?"

"A few more pages. I saw a few problems when I was at the session. Anna should have caught those."

"Anna?"

"I rely on her to proofread."

"And then she gives them back to you?"

"Yeah."

Note: the manager does not need to push further concerning the proofreading. Jim realizes his finger-pointing excuse fell apart.

"You mentioned the Lantry materials met the client's need. Tell me more about what you consider an acceptable level of handouts for that type of session."

"I would have done more but ran out of time."

The manager realizes Jim thinks he can use a "time is the culprit" excuse and decides to switch tactics and head straight to what matters to a proud, charismatic trainer. "How do you want to be known by our clients?"

"The best trainer they've ever seen."

"How close are you to reaching that goal?" The manager's tone is genuine, giving Jim the sense that the manager buys in to the importance of this goal.

"Some think I am."

"What's getting in your way of everyone thinking it?"

"Time."

"Is that all?"

The employee lowers his eyes. *"I have to give 100-percent."*

"That puzzles me."

The employee looks startled.

"You give 100-percent when you're in front of a group. Explain how come you don't give that level of effort ahead of time."

"I don't know. I didn't think of it that way.'

"Let me give you a chance to reflect on that. For now, tell me about the handout packets you'll create for next two sessions."

"Error-free. I'll review them. Anna proofreads, but she won't understand the concepts enough to catch problems I need to catch. They'll have a depth of quality information so that the client feels they received more than expected for their money."

"Can you put a number guideline for how many pages that is for an hour of training?"

"I'll go back to my last several months of training sessions and calculate how many handout pages used per hour of training."

"And from the client's point of view, what does the handout packet the trainer leaves behind mean?"

"It's a resource of what was covered. They can turn back to it."

"That's another area I'd like you to more fully consider."

"Got it."

"I appreciate you and this discussion. Let's meet next Thursday at ten, so you can tell me about giving 100-percent during session preparation."

Follow-up: When they met, Jim told the manager that he had felt his engaging delivery "made up" for handout package deficiencies. He felt that clients paid to see him in action. He realized that if he wanted to be the best trainer clients had ever seen, he had to go beyond that and leave polished training handout packets that clients would see as valuable.

Reset complete. Coaching, however, had only just begun. For more on "coaching," see the next chapter.

CHAPTER 8

Coaching Your Employees to Increased Accountability

In this chapter, you will learn how to coach your employees, deepening their engagement, job satisfaction, commitment, and personal and professional accountability. By making coaching a regular part of your organization's culture, you maximize your employees' potential and fully integrate them into your organization.

Coaching in a Nutshell

If you have played or been around sports or competitive activities such as football, soccer, track, or debate, you know firsthand the difference coaching makes. Coaches help players optimize their performance.

If you have competed individually or on a team with a coach's guidance, you have felt what it means to work with a coach who believes in you. When your coach said, "you can do more," you dug deep into yourself and accomplished results beyond those you had believed possible.

Players work hard to learn from and please coaches who believe in them. While employees occasionally bristle when a supervisor says, "try that another way," when coaches say, "do that differently," players listen carefully and follow the coach's counsel. Players sense that their coaches and they are on the same team and share the same goals.

In a business environment, experienced, savvy managers coach employees by providing guidance beyond what a manager normally gives an employee. Manager coaches serve as mentors, role models, and advisors, helping employees learn the mindset, skills, and strategies they need to excel.

Coaching Benefits

Coaching ensures players are not left to sink or swim but rather adds a fast lane on which employees travel. When coaches provide the skills, strategies, and methods employees need to increase their proficiency and grow in their careers, it engages and enables employees to excel. Coaching increases employees' job satisfaction, morale, and loyalty leading to higher retention and accountability.

Leaders that coach rather than command employees skillfully build an agile workplace in which employees self-manage, creating a healthy, growing, profitable organization. Coaching additionally helps employees put setbacks into perspective, a necessary support during challenging times such as those experienced in 2020 with COVID-19.

Coaching Has Become More Important Than Ever

A coaching culture makes a workplace attractive to prospective employees. Employees see career development as job security and look for and stay with organizations willing to invest in them. Believing skills acquisition provides them both job security and career growth, they look for an organization willing to invest in them. LinkedIn's 2020 Workplace Learning Report[1] revealed that 94 percent of employees say they would stay at a company longer if it invested in their career development.

The Manager as Coach

Here is how to increase your coaching proficiency and success.

Intentionally Program Time Into Your Calendar

Intentionally set aside time in your calendar to coach and provide your employees with motivational and constructive feedback. Your employees want to learn how you are assessing their performance, what they are doing well, and where they need to improve.

---

[1] https://hbr.org/2018/06/96-of-u-s-professionals-say-they-need-flexibility-but-only-47-have-it

In the worksite, manager coaches frequently arrive at work early or leave late. The manager's physical presence helps employees see the manager's commitment and gives the manager/coach opportunities for informal discussions with others at the beginning or end of the workday.

Manager coaches often find that some employees intentionally arrive early or remain late to connect with them. When you are a manager coach that departs later than the norm, it also gives you a chance to drop by others' workstations and informally chat, recognizing and reinforcing their commitment.

If your team works remotely, you can accomplish the same objectives by scheduling informal, relaxed discussions after your employees finish important projects or tasks, as employees will welcome the chance to debrief you on their accomplishments.

You Are a Role Model

What you do speaks louder than what you say. Always remember that employees watch you to learn how they can become leaders. Coaching includes instilling values and tailoring an employee's mindset toward accountability. Regularly ask yourself: what kind of example do I set?

Fully Involve Your Coached Employee From the Start

Coaching your employee begins with your goals for the employee within your organization, combined with the employee's starting point and where s/he wants to grow. You might ask your employee:

- "Where do you see your role evolving in our organization?"
- "What do you hope to gain from our coaching discussions?"
- "What skills or capabilities do you need to feel more successful in your current assignments?"
- "How do you best like to receive feedback and what kind of feedback is most helpful?"

Additionally, you will want to get to know your employee as a person in terms of his/her job-related motivations. A simple tool is to give your employee a stack of 17 cards, each with a different word or phrase on it and to ask your employee to stack the cards from top to bottom in terms of what most matters to him/her in a job.

The words/phrases: advancement; learning; work/life balance; autonomy; challenge; variety; chance to make a difference; collaboration with great teammates; achievement; security; seeing an idea through to completion; money; status; chance to lead; other; other; other. The three "other" cards give your employee the opportunity to write what is most important to him/her but is not included on the other 14 cards.

Because all the words/phrases may be desired in a job, asking your employee to rank them in order of importance gives you, and occasionally your employee, a clear picture for what drives him/her to succeed.

Keep the Goal in View

When asked what made him such a great hockey player, Wayne Gretsky responded, "I skate to where the puck will be." Continue to focus your employee on the goal and what s/he can gain and become through continued learning and hard work. Set employees up for success by providing them increased challenges within their limits, but that stretch them so that they, like Gretsky, can proactively see and take advantage of opportunities that advance themselves and the company.

Adjust Your Coaching to Your Employee

Coaching is not a one-size-fits-all program. The best coaches use different styles for different employees based on their motivations and their communication and learning style. Some employees need more instruction and constructive criticism than others. Others respond better to being provided increasingly complex assignments along with access to a skilled mentor who they can call when they run into a snag or want a sounding board.

Instill Confidence

Instill your employees with confidence. Look for opportunities to recognize each employee for strong performance and extra effort. Coaching comments such as "that's good work" and "that's a great idea" mean a lot. Set your employees up for continued success by pushing them to learn, grow, and stretch and then congratulating them when they do.

Do Not Take Over

While you might be tempted to take over part or all of a project that is moving slowly or in the wrong direction, remember that employees learn through experience. Provide them guidance instead whether in-person, via Zoom, or by e-mail or text.

If you find yourself "telling" your employee what to do and how to do it, remember that questions spark insights and give employees the sense they "did it themselves."

Encourage Employees to Walk Through Your Open Door

It is not enough to tell employees you have an open door. Some, particularly those who want to seem competent in your eyes, will not walk in. Reach out to them; imagine that you are leaning out the door with your hand stretched forward, until they learn they can voice concerns or ask you for advice and assistance without penalty.

When you and your employee finish your discussion, thank your employee for trusting you by sharing their thoughts with you and close the discussion with, "I hope you'll again feel free to initiate these conversations in the future."

Create Goals

Show your employees that you value them enough to take an active interest in their career and professional success. Work with each employee to create professional goals aligned with your organization's goals and a game plan for achieving them. Keep your employees accountable for their improvement by scheduling time to meet with each to review their growth and accomplishments, and to plan their next steps. Employee goal-setting easily aligns with organizational succession planning as you and your employee can develop stair-step goals to positions of increased responsibility.

Coach Tools

Your primary coaching tools include:

1. Questions
2. Feedback
3. Recognition
4. 360-degree reviews

Coaching Questions

Questioning Technique

As discussed in Chapter 3, start your questions with words and phrases such as "what," "how," "tell me more," and "could you discuss (or share or explain)" instead of "why" or "did." "Why" and "did" words create defensiveness, justification, and shut down otherwise productive coaching discussions.

Consider how questions such as "why are you behind schedule?"; "why did you do that?"; or "didn't you know better than that?" would impact you. Contrast those questions with "What have you done this week that worked well?"; "what do you want to improve?"; "what can we or you do differently to get even better results?"

Next, train yourself to hear "signal" words, words that signify valuable information lurks below the surface and ask questions that delve deeper. For example, what jumps out at you if you coach an employee who says, "I want to start new initiatives and work on them from start to finish. I want to be placed in a team leadership role. I think I'd get a charge out of leading a team." As a coach, I would ask, "Is there a new initiative you have in mind?"

The following sections offer specific questions to spark your coaching sessions.

Career Development Questions

In your initial coaching sessions, you have asked your employee:

- "In what areas do you want to grow to better achieve your professional and career goals?"

- "Where do you want to be one, two and three years from now in your professional growth?"

Continued development questions inspire employees to imagine a clearer, more exciting role in your organization. Effective questions include:

- "How would you feel if you took on _____?"
- "What projects would you like to work on or be more involved in?"
- "What makes you our best candidate to tackle _____?"
- "Is there a project you'd like to try but you haven't had the time or resources? What is it about that project that intrigues you? How would tackling it benefit our organization or you personally?"
- "What other roles in our organization do you find interesting? What skills do those roles require that you would like to develop?"
- "What else can I do to support you attaining increased job satisfaction or progress in your career?"

Focusing Your Employee on Self-Management

Questions help focus your employees on accountable self-assessment. Effective questions include:

- "What is working in what you're now doing (in project "x")?"
- "What is contributing to your effectiveness in producing the results you intend?"
- "In what areas are you pleased with your work quality?"
- "What are you doing that creates high-quality deliverables?"
- "How can you make your processes even more effective and efficient?"
- "What can you do better or differently to get even stronger results?"
- "That's a great idea; is there anything else you or I can do?"
- "If you were your own manager, what would you ask yourself to work on or do better?"

- "How do you propose putting your plan into action?"
- "How do you plan to accomplish that?"
- "If you were your own manager, how would you evaluate your progress?"

Questions to Focus Employees on Learning, Continuous Improvement, and Accountability

Questions inspire introspection and deeper learning. Effective questions include:

- "What have you learned on this project (this week)?"
- "If you tried this approach, what do you think might result?" After your employee responds, you can add, "Please experiment with it and let me know how it works."
- "What other methods have you tried? How have they worked?"
- "If that doesn't work, what could you next try?"
- "Do you feel fully utilized? In what other areas would you like to contribute?"
- "How can you or others on your team better support one another?"
- "Are you getting enough feedback from me and others on your work or are there areas in which you would like more feedback?"

Partnering Questions

You build the strongest coaching and manager-to-employee bond when you partner with your employees. The following questions prove effective in engaging your employees to improve your leadership effectiveness, their work, and your organization.

- "What has been a work highlight this month?"
- "What has been a lowlight?"
- "What's one thing we can do to improve the performance of our team?"

- "If you were managing the team, what would you do differently?"
- "What thoughts or questions do you have about our future as a company?"
- "What needs to change in our team meetings?"
- "What are your thoughts about our one-on-one meetings? How would you like to improve them?" or, "How can we improve how our team works together?"
- "What have you learned from teams working remotely that contributed to better communication, collaboration and accountability?"
- "In what ways could I better help you be more effective and successful?"
- "Would you like more or less direction from me on your work?"
- "What's a problem we have on our team that I might not know about?"
- "If you were the business owner, what's the first thing you'd change?"
- "What's something a past manager of yours did that inspired you?" "That demotivated you?"
- "What's one recommendation you'd make to improve our workplace culture?"
- "For you, what's the best aspect of working here?"
- "What is one thing I could experiment with doing differently?"
- "What's an example of a situation you feel I've handled well? What about one you would have wanted me to handle differently—what was it and what could I have done?"

When you hear your employee's answers to the above questions, remember that coaching goes both ways. While all of us want to hear that everything is going well, be prepared to learn that at least one employee wants you to upgrade your coaching techniques.

Questioning to Inspire Soloists to Collaborate

Your coaching questions help you turn soloists into collaborative team players. Effective questions that address this include:

- "What do you depend on others for in terms of communicating, coordinating, and support?"
- "What do they depend on you for?"
- "How effectively do you collaborate with/support your peers?"
- "How could you become a more effective collaborator?"
- "What does your department/team do well to communicate/collaborate/coordinate with other teams?"
- "What does your department/team need to do better to become an even more effective collaborator?"
- "What do you need to do to become an even more accountable collaborator?"
- "What does your department/team need to do better to become even more collaborative?"
- "How does our entire organization rate as an organization in which we collaborate across teams/departments and divisions?"

Using Questioning to Turn Problems into Learning Opportunities

Let us assume your employee fell off the accountability wagon three to four weeks ago or with one solo or team project. You have e-mailed your employee and asked that they meet you in your office or call you via Zoom or another videoconference method. What thoughts do you think run through their mind as they near your office door or presses connect on the meeting icon?

They probably think, I messed up; I'm going to get chewed out.

Given that, what questions should you ask him/her?

Ask your employee to brief you concerning the situation: "Hi, I understand project X didn't go as planned. Can you tell me about that?"

If your employee provides only the Cliff's notes version, ask him/her more questions; however, do not initially turn them into teaching moments. You want your employee to know you do not plan to chew them out, but instead want him/her to explain what went wrong and how they could have executed the assignment more effectively.

Next, ask "what did you learn?" or "what would you do differently if you could go back in time?"

Then ask, "how can you fix this?" or "how can you make the best of the current situation?" Remain solution-oriented and you will have turned a problem into learning and growth.

Feedback

Coaches provide employees with realistic, accurate performance-oriented feedback that motivates and corrects. Effective feedback comes from a genuine desire to help and adheres to the following guidelines.

"Tee up" before you give feedback. Let your employee start the conversation by asking him/her how things are going before you offer your views.

Be your employee's friend in the foxhole; be willing to deliver the hard truth when necessary, but without a judgmental, parental sting. Whatever you say, say it straightforwardly and respectfully so that your delivery does not bury your message.

Make your feedback performance-based, rather than personal; speak to what happened or needs to happen. A statement such as, "I want you to offer two suggestions in our next meeting" provides helpful coaching while "you need to show more initiative" does not.

Give specifics, especially when giving positive feedback. "It was really effective when you concisely described all three components in three short paragraphs" is more helpful than "great job."

Focus your feedback on behavior your employee can change. "I want you to greet customers with a smile" gives a shy employee a task s/he can manage, in contrast with "you need to get over your shyness."

Give your feedback as immediately as possible. If you procrastinate, an employee's irksome habits may become ingrained. At the same time, do not "hit and run" coach by giving feedback before you have taken a moment to think "how do I word this for best results?"

Because most people hear negative comments more loudly than positive ones, as in how loudly the "but" sounds in "you're nice, but…," you create a more effective balance by offering three to five positive comments to every constructively critical comment you make.

Focus your feedback on results. As presented in chapters 6 and 7, provide feedback phrased as expectation guidance rather than problem delineation.

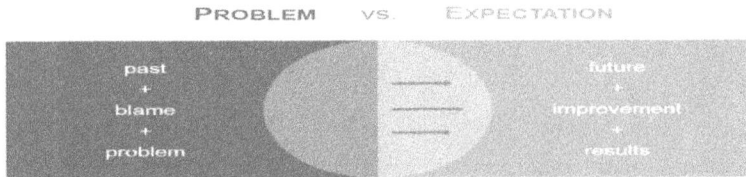

Figure 8.1 Problem versus expectation

Recognition

If you have played team sports, you have experienced how your coach started each game with encouragement and provided half-time pep talks even when your team had fewer points on the board than the opposing team. Recognition of what your employee does well can be a springboard into how they can improve.

Employees need encouragement and recognition commensurate with their efforts. At the same time, only make positive statements you mean, as inauthentic praise never rings true.

Recognition becomes even more important in difficult times, as positives mitigate stress. You have likely heard that most employees crave the effects of a highly addictive chemical. When they receive too little of this chemical, they may feel anxious or more easily frustrated. With increases of this chemical, they feel pleasure. The chemical is dopamine.

Dopamine stimulates the areas of the brain that produce positive emotions such as satisfaction. Evolutionary biologists credit dopamine with aiding humans' ability to learn as individuals that experience a dopamine charge after completing a successful activity generally return for an additional dopamine surge. Although some individuals turn to alcohol and drugs to feel dopamine production, receiving recognition for good work releases dopamine and cements the understanding that similar continued behaviors will lead to additional recognition, praise, and dopamine.

Finally, strong leaders and coaches celebrate successes with their players and team. Leaders often focus so intensely on achievement that when their employees and teams achieve milestones, the leader rewards them with the next assignment. Ask yourself, "What was the last time that you met with an employee or your team to celebrate their recent successes?" If you cannot remember or it was longer than six weeks ago, schedule a celebration.

360-Degree Review

360-degree reviews prove invaluable in convincing employees to make changes and identifying where employees need coaching. A 360-degree review provides you and your employee with clear, concise information concerning the employee's strengths and the areas needing improvement.

Here is how the 360-degree review works. Seven to 11 individuals receive a form asking for confidential, detailed information in 12 to 18 areas concerning the employee.

You or your human resource (HR) officer or consultant receives the responses, follows up with phone calls to ask further questions, and compiles a detailed summary of everything provided by at least two or more of the respondents. Because the individual writing the report uses their own words and uses a "two-person bar" (only information voiced by two or more of those surveyed is included), those who give comments receive a reasonable measure of confidentiality.

Useful questions include the following six, with a full set of 18 provided in Figure 8.2.

"How does this employee handle leadership and present him/herself as a role model?"

"What can you say about how this employee works with people?"

"What can you say about how this employee makes 'judgement calls?'"

"What can you say about this employee's work ethic?'

"Do you trust this employee?"

"What do you wish this employee would do differently?"

1. How does _____ handle leadership and present him/herself as a role model?

2. What can you say about how _____ works with his/her employees and how s/he manages?

3. In what ways does this employee demonstrate accountability? Are there areas in which s/he needs to show a greater degree of accountability, and if so, could you elaborate?

4. What can you say about how _____ works with his/her peers and how s/he collaborates with others?

5. What can you say about how _____ works with other senior managers in the company?

6. What can you tell me about how _____ communicates (both orally and in writing; both in giving information and in listening/receiving feedback)?

7. How does _____ handle conflict and individuals who hold a different view than s/he does? How does s/he handle problems?

8. How does _____ bring out the best in his/her team?

9. How does _____ interact with clients?

10. What can you tell me about the quality of how _____ makes decisions and functions in the area of making "judgment calls?"

11. What can you say about _____'s work product?

12. What can you say about _____'s work ethic and how _____ "steps up to the plate?"

13. Is _____ a person you trust? Is s/he honest? Does s/he walk the talk?

14. Is _____ fair and reasonable?

15. Is _____ organized and someone who follows up on projects?

16. What are _____'s Achilles' heels?

17. What do you wish _____ would do differently?

18. What is _____'s role in your organization and on an overall basis how well does s/he fulfill his/her role?

Figure 8.2 360-degree review questions

Here is a sample of what you might learn:

How Does Mr./Ms. Sample Handle Leadership and Present Him/ Herself as a Role Model?

Five of the eight interviewees state that they did not view Mr./Ms. Sample as a leader or even someone interested in leadership. Two interviewees commented that Mr./Ms. Sample needs to realize s/he leads (or does not) by example, and when s/he refuses to accept accountability for his/her errors, instead blaming others, s/he loses their respect. *(The actual review will contain several additional paragraphs.)*

What Can You Say Concerning How Mr./Ms. Sample Works With People?

Four of the eight interviewees commented that Mr./Ms. Sample responds defensively to even constructively worded criticism. *(The actual review will contain several additional paragraphs.)*

What Can You Say About Mr./Ms. Sample's Work Product?

Seven of the eight interviewees described Mr./Ms. Sample's work product as excellent or high quality. Although these seven interviewees view Mr./ Ms. Sample as an extremely capable, hard worker, three of them noted that Mr./Ms. Sample does not get material to them on time, due to his/her "perfectionist reworking of details."

As you can imagine, it is invaluable to your organization when your employees receive candid feedback from their peers and direct reports, motivating them to change in significant, needed ways.

Figure 8.2 provides you a list of eighteen key areas to include in your 360-degree reviews.

CHAPTER 9

Retaining Your Top Talent

This chapter offers you proven strategies for retaining your top talent. You will also learn to avoid the missteps that lead even good employers to lose their best employees.

Turnover Costs

Unwanted turnover costs employers a substantial amount in lost money, knowledge, and productivity. Multiple researchers estimate that losing an employee costs an employer 90 to 200 percent of the employee's annual salary.[1] This financial burden includes the time and expenses involved in recruiting, onboarding, and training a new hire.

The employer also loses institutional knowledge and productivity as it takes 6 to 12 months or longer for a new hire to come up to speed. Crucial projects are often halted, or start over from the beginning as other employees pick up the slack. Research also links high turnover rates to organizational performance shortfalls. As one example, a study involving 333 hospitals revealed that nurse turnover accounted for 68 percent of the variability in per-bed operating costs.[2]

Morale also takes a hit when a well-liked, well-respected employee departs and a gap opens in the team dynamic. The employee's former coworkers begin to wonder if they should look around as well. The departing employee may tell those he or she has left behind how exciting their new position/organization is, or even solicit them to join the new company.

---

[1] https://shrm.org/hr-today/trends-and-forecasting/special-reports-and-expert-views/Documents/Retaining-Talent.pdf

[2] Alexander, J., J. Bloom, and B. Nuchols. 1994. "Nursing Turnover and Hospital Efficiency: An Organization-Level Analysis." *Industrial Relations* 33, pp. 505–520.

Why Employees Leave

Employees leave organizations for all kinds of reasons. Some grow bored in their job as initially interesting challenges start to taste like well-chewed bubble gum. Others take stock of their professional lives and realize they are in the wrong profession or industry and seek a change before they invest more time.

Some receive solicitations from those who have found them on LinkedIn forums. Others screen websites like Indeed.com monthly, viewing it as a candy land of new opportunities. Some follow a spouse transferred to a different location. Life events such as a new child, a marriage or divorce, or the illness of a loved family member lead some employees to change priorities and resign.

Some employees grow bitter when passed over for a promotion or when a teammate they dislike receives an opportunity they felt should have been theirs. Others choose to leave rather than resolve a festering conflict with a supervisor or coworker. As described in Chapter 4, first year churn can lead to turnover if your recently hired employee receives a more enticing job offer soon after s/he joins your organization.

Stop Unwanted Turnover *Before* It Occurs

Managing for Accountability gives you the tools, strategies, framework, and skills you need to prevent unwanted turnover. The following provides a quick reminder of what you have already learned that directly targets retention.

In chapters 2 and 3, you gained the tools you need to hire the right employees, ones that will find their work in your organization interesting, enjoyable, meaningful, and challenging. You learned how to effectively onboard your new employees so that they feel competent. You received information on how to create a positive and vibrant workplace culture that increases employee job satisfaction.

Retention primarily rests on an effective relationship with an employee's immediate supervisor and in Chapter 4, you learned how to develop a solid connection with your new employee and how to uncover trouble before it grows roots.

In Chapter 5, you developed skills and strategies for inspiring your employees to buy-in to your organization's mission and vision and a framework for a motivating reward system.

Because connected employees hesitate to leave coworkers they enjoy working with, the team development skills you learned in Chapter 6 directly address retention.

Your next steps and strategies include:

- Targeting exactly what each employee needs to stay satisfied and engaged.
- Giving your employees the opportunity to raise concerns before they become deal-breakers.
- Ensuring you have a compensation system your employees consider just.
- Providing your employees with the flexibility they need to have a work/life balance by allowing compressed work weeks, job sharing, sabbaticals, and early departures on sunny or snowy Fridays. Recent research documents that employees with a good work/life balance are 10 percent more likely to remain with their companies.[3]
- Ensuring your employees feel recognized and valued.
- Providing your employees with career and professional development opportunities.
- Effectively handling crises such as a significant client loss or pandemic.

The best tool in your retention arsenal: the stay interview

If you have ever been blindsided by a valuable employee's resignation and conducted an exit interview, you may have asked the right questions six months too late.

Like autopsies, exit interviews detail why employees leave your organization. By contrast, stay interviews are superior, in that they help you retain valued employees by giving you a clear picture of what each

---

[3] https://tinypulse.com/hubfs/2018%20Employee%20Retention%20Report.pdf

employee needs to stay fully engaged. These interviews prove so valuable that wise employers start them at the end of each employer's first month and repeat them every several months.

Stay interviews uncover what really matters for each key employee— is it a raise, decision-making autonomy, challenging work, or knowing their supervisor considers them on an upward trajectory? You do not want to guess at your employee's motivations and reward your employee with a raise when what s/he craves is work/life balance, the chance to learn something new, or the freedom to work from home for part of the workweek.

Stay interviews show your employee you care, leading your employee to feel highly valued and increasingly bonded to you and your organization.

Stay interviews give you an opportunity to find out what will keep your employee working their hardest, and what might lead them to leave. You cannot fix problems you do not know exist, but they can cost you, particularly if your employee already cruises job search platforms looking for new opportunities.

A stay interview may reveal an employee that you believed satisfied wants to progress faster or beyond what he or she sees as achievable within your company, when if you knew that situation existed, you could have provided ways for the employee to gain additional skill and responsibility while remaining in your company.

Stay interviews also boost productivity by giving owners and managers the ability to address factors that significantly increase employee discretionary effort and retention—before the employee hits the exit ramp.

Conducting the Stay Interview

Begin your stay interview by saying, "I want to talk with you today about the key reasons you stay with us, because we want our organization to have a great and satisfying work environment. My goal is to learn what I can do to make us an employer of choice for you in areas we can control."

For best results, you need to ask easily answered questions on hard topics. Employees may not honestly answer "have you ever thought about leaving the company?" for fear it may make them appear less dedicated or result in other ramifications. Instead, try "if you won the Publishers

Clearinghouse sweepstakes and decided to leave us, what would you miss most and least?" or "if you could change anything about your current job or our company, what would you change?"

During the interview, really listen and do not attempt to guide the conversation toward what you want to hear or defend the status quo. Although you will want to follow-up each interview with strategies that meet your employee's needs, do not turn the interview into a negotiation session as that can muddy the waters, particularly if your employee asks for benefits or events you cannot deliver.

Similarly, do not combine stay interviews with performance reviews. Your approach in the stay interview is to listen and fully understand what motivates, inspires, and frustrates your employee. In the performance review, your approach combines listening to your employee with providing an improvement-oriented assessment of your employee's performance, along with recognition for your employee's achievements.

What if you learn you cannot give an employee what the employee most desires? Be honest. Stay interviewees produce good results even when all you can do is demonstrate you care and will do what you can to explore options. Finally, expect to spend 30 minutes on each stay interview, a minor investment, given the significant results they produce. This list gives you 25 stay interview questions, allowing you to select the 7 to 10 questions you can use each time you conduct a stay interview:

During your stay interview, take notes. Then, review your notes regularly and ask yourself what you have done to keep your employee motivated, engaged, and positively challenged according to what they revealed in the interview.

Give Your Employees the Opportunity to Raise Concerns

You want your employees to feel they can safely come to you with concerns before they become deal-breakers or coworker grumblings and to believe that you will provide honest answers to their questions. You developed the foundation for this in Chapter 4 and also learned tools, such as the all-hands meeting, "management by walking around," and skip-level meetings to give employees platforms for safely voicing their thoughts.

1. When you leave work each day and think "that was a great day," what is it that made a "great day" for you?
2. How does your job measure up to what I promised when we first met? Are there ways in which we need to course-correct?
3. What might entice you away from our organization?
4. What is it that you are glad to have found here, that you sense will keep you engaged and satisfied?
5. What about your job makes you jump out of bed in the morning?
6. What do you like best/least about your job?
7. How does the workplace and schedule work for you? Is there anything we need to adjust?
8. What most surprises you about our organization's culture?
9. What is something new you want to learn this year?
10. Is there anything you would like to change about your job or department?
11. What is one thing that would make your job more satisfying and rewarding?
12. When you travel to work each day, what are you looking forward to?
13. How does working here compare to what you thought it would be like?
14. What do you know now that you wish you had known earlier? What has been a pleasant surprise?
15. Is there one person in the organization who has really been helpful to you of late (so that we can thank them appropriately)?
16. How do you like to be rewarded? Recognized?
17. What kind of support or direction do you need from me? What do you need that you are not getting?
18. If you had a friend considering working here, what would you tell your friend?
19. If you had a magic wand, what would be one thing you could change about this organization?
20. In what areas do you wish you could get more feedback? More praise? More improvement-oriented feedback?
21. What can I/we do to support your career goals?
22. As your manager, what could I do a little more or a little less of? Or, start doing or stop doing?
23. How can I help you to feel more successful at work?
24. What work challenges do you most enjoy? What new challenges would you most like to tackle?
25. What is a job goal you have set for yourself?

Figure 9.1 Great stay interview questions

The other ingredient key to surfacing concerns is trust, which rests on honesty, openness, and demonstrated leadership. If you would like to assess whether your employees trust you, complete this self-assessment, scoring yourself 0 to 7 in each area. You can also ask your human relations representative or a neutral, third-party consultant to confidentially collect your employees' views in these areas:

This leader (*please rate on a scale of 0 to 7*):

- Keeps confidences
- Is a straight shooter who communicates honestly and openly
- Supports us and has our backs
- Follows through on what s/he commits to
- Provides leadership we can trust
- Walks his/her talk
- Is authentic; we know what to expect from him/her
- Keeps us in the know about what is going on in the organization
- Is fair
- Respects us by asking us for our ideas and regularly acts on what we say

If your self-assessment or what you learn from your employees' assessment of you in the trust area shows deficiencies, you will want to immediately address the pinpointed deficits through executive coaching or another mechanism.

A Just Compensation System Keeps Accountable Employees

Is your organization competitive in terms of salaries, bonuses, paid time off, professional developmental opportunities, health benefits, retirement plans, and intangible forms of compensation such as the opportunity to work remotely? If not, you risk your accountable employees leaving for better offers.

If you offer competitive compensation, make sure your employees realize it by communicating your total rewards package, including tangible and intangible benefits. Intangible benefits might include the opportunities you provide for upward mobility, flexible work hours, and professional development.

Additionally, you can tie reward to retention, by providing long-term employees with additional vacation hours, the potential for stock options, and by linking defined benefit plan payouts to years of service.

Flexibility and Work/Life Balance Increase the Retention of Accountable Employees

In a *Harvard Business Review* survey of 1,583 white-collar professionals, 96 percent said they needed flexibility, yet only 47 percent reported having the flexibility needed—a gap of 54 percent[4]. According to the HBR study, employees lacking flexibility were twice as likely to report dissatisfaction. A full half of the 1,583 white-collar professionals surveyed stated that they would leave their employers if offered a more flexible alternative.[5]

Deloitte and Touche's internal research puts bottom-line numbers to the importance flexibility plays in retention. Their data reveals a $41.5M savings in employee turnover costs by retaining employees that stated they would have left if they had not been able to work a flexible schedule.[6]

According to a 2018 survey by FlexJobs, 80 percent of employees surveyed reported that they would choose a job offering a flexible schedule over one that did not. These employees also stated that they would feel more loyal to employers that provided a flexible work schedule. Additionally, 35 percent of surveyed employees stated that they prioritized a flexible work schedule over a more prestigious position, and 30 percent reported that they placed a higher value on a flexible work schedule than on additional vacation time.[7]

The FlexJobs survey also reported that 30 percent of those surveyed had left their jobs because their employer did not offer flexible work

---

[4] https://hbr.org/2018/06/96-of-u-s-professionals-say-they-need-flexibility-but-only-47-have-it

[5] https://hbr.org/2018/06/96-of-u-s-professionals-say-they-need-flexibility-but-only-47-have-it

[6] https://hiring.monster.com/employer-resources/workforce-management/employee-performance/employee-engagement-ideas/

[7] https://flexjobs.com/employer-blog/the-benefits-of-allowing-employees-a-flexible-schedule/

options; another 16 percent were job-hunting due to a lack of flexible options.[8]

Balancing Personal Challenges During Pandemics

Employees need to know their managers understand that they have lives outside of work, particularly during a global pandemic or other personal crisis. COVID-19 has led many employees to feel stretched past their breaking point by the need to assist their children with alternate remote or home schooling while working eight hours a day between eight and five. According to a recent *Harvard Business Review* study, 33 percent of more than 1,500 employees surveyed reported that the "normal" workday structure made it challenging for them to be the type of parent they want to be.[9] As just one example, critical work meetings may occur simultaneously with school district technology glitches, and a parent may then feel torn between helping their children and meeting their employer's expectations. COVID-19 has made supporting working parents an employer necessity.

Employees without children benefit as well from scheduling flexibility and the opportunity to work remotely, which gives them the ability to be home when the plumber arrives or an ill family member needs care.

Flexibility Benefits Cost Little

What does it cost employers to offer employees flexibility? Often, **zero.** Consider the following solutions:

- **Remote work.** Allow your employees to work off-site for part or all their work week, saving them commuting time.
- **Unconventional hours.** Allow your employees to reorder their working hours to create a schedule that works best

---

[8] https://flexjobs.com/employer-blog/the-benefits-of-allowing-employees-a-flexible-schedule/

[9] https://hbr.org/2018/06/96-of-u-s-professionals-say-they-need-flexibility-but-only-47-have-it

for them and optimizes productivity and performance for your organization. For employees home-schooling children, this means work done before the kids wake up, in snatches throughout the school day, and after the kids finish dinner. For commuting employees, this may mean a 7 a.m. to 3 p.m. work schedule to shave off as much as an hour from rush hour commute time.

According to a study reported in businessnewsdaily. com, 26 percent of employees stated that the freedom to choose when they start and end their shifts is one of the two flexible workplace policies that employees desire most (the other is the ability to choose their work location).[10]

- **Guilt-free stepping away.** Grant your employees the ability to step away from portions of their workday, marking them off so that they can schedule time helping their school-age children or taking care of personal needs.
- **Reduced workload with a part-time schedule/reduced workload.** Allow employees unable to work full time the ability to work a part-time schedule, or enable job sharing and gain two minds synergistically tackling one role.
- **Alternative schedules.** Consider instituting flextime or compressed work weeks, such as allowing employees to take Fridays off in the summer or allowing employees to work an extra hour on Thursdays so that they can leave at 4 p.m. in the summer on Fridays.

Flexibility Offers Employers Benefits in Addition to Retention

Productivity

According to the *Harvard Business Review* survey of 1,583 white-collar professionals, a lack of flexibility may lower performance and productivity for one-third of the workforce; 34 percent of those surveyed reported

---

[10] https://businessnewsdaily.com/10108-employee-flexibility-recruiting.html

that the traditional workday structure made it challenging for them to sustainably perform to employer expectations[6].

According to a remote collaborative workers assessment conducted by CoSo Cloud, 77 percent of remote workers show higher productivity than their workplace-bound employees.[11] Of these employees, 30 percent completed more work in less time than in the office, and another 24 percent of employees completed more work in the same amount of time.[12]

A two-year study conducted on U.S. Patent and Trademark Office employees noted that employees allowed to work remotely were 4.4 percent more productive than their in-office counterparts.[13]

Global Workplace Analytics reported that Compaq's flexible workforce increased productivity between 15 and 45 percent and noted that American Express' flexible workforce achieved a productivity level 43 percent higher than their traditional counterparts.[14]

Employees provided workday flexibility by their employers feel trusted, respected, and valued, and often work extra weekend hours as a "payback" to their employers who allow them to take time out during the traditional workweek. Global Workplace Analytics reported that AT&T discovered that its remote workers worked five more hours weekly than its office workers.[15]

FlexJob's 2019 survey of remote employees revealed that they worked 1.4 more days monthly or 16.8 more workdays per year than did their in-office counterparts.[16]

Recruitment and Other Longevity Benefits

A flexible work policy additionally provides employers a no-cost way to make their total employee compensation package stand out and enables

---

[11] https://businessnewsdaily.com/10108-employee-flexibility-recruiting.html

[12] https://peoplescout.com/insights/flexibility-in-the-workplace-2/

[13] https://flexjobs.com/employer-blog/the-benefits-of-allowing-employees-a-flexible-schedule/

[14] https://peoplescout.com/insights/flexibility-in-the-workplace-2/

[15] https://peoplescout.com/insights/flexibility-in-the-workplace-2/

[16] https://flexjobs.com/employer-blog/the-benefits-of-allowing-employees-a-flexible-schedule/

them to attract top-tier employees who are specifically looking for or can only handle a flexible or part-time work schedule.

In a study conducted by ManpowerGroup Solutions, nearly 40 percent of job candidates (worldwide) reported that schedule flexibility was one of the top three factors they used when making career decisions.[17]

Employers experience other benefits, including fewer missed days of work and retained institutional knowledge. Employees too sick to go into the office can often get some work done from home. Further, employees who no longer want to work full time or to live in certain climates or locations can continue working for employers that allow flexible and remote work.[18]

Feeling Valued; Being Recognized Keeps Accountable Employees

According to a Reward Gateway survey, 70 percent of employees stated that "motivation and morale would improve 'massively' with managers saying thank you more" often.[19] According to other studies, 69 percent of employees would work harder if they felt their efforts were better appreciated.[20] The Aberdeen Group's research confirms this, with 60 percent of best-in-class organizations reporting that employee recognition is extremely valuable in driving employee performance.[21]

Yet, many employers do not provide ample recognition. According to Gallup research, 68 percent of employees have not received any form of recognition for good work in the past year.[22]

---

[17] https://businessnewsdaily.com/10108-employee-flexibility-recruiting.html

[18] https://businessnewsdaily.com/10108-employee-flexibility-recruiting.html

[19] https://benefitnews.com/news/workers-willing-to-leave-a-job-if-not-praised-enough

[20] https://semoscloud.com/blog/5-reasons-why-you-should-recognize-your-employees-work/

[21] https://semoscloud.com/blog/5-reasons-why-you-should-recognize-your-employees-work/

[22] https://semoscloud.com/blog/5-reasons-why-you-should-recognize-your-employees-work/

According to studies by Bersin & Associates, 66 percent of employees are likely to leave their jobs if they feel unappreciated.[23] Reward Gateway's research reveals similar results, reporting that nearly one in two surveyed employees would leave a company where they did not feel appreciated.[24] According to another study, 21.5 percent of employees that did not feel recognized when they did great work had interviewed for a job in the past three months, in contrast to 12.4 percent that did feel recognized.[25]

If you are like many managers who thrive on achieving goals without needing others to notice what you have accomplished, you appreciate good performance but do not say so as often as you could. As a result, your employees may feel taken for granted.

Managers who pay attention to their employees see many opportunities to give them recognition and make them feel valued. This personalized attention creates and maintains the emotional bond between employees, the manager, and the organization.

Consider how easy it might be to take time today to tell your employees what you genuinely appreciate about how they handle their workload: "Thank you," "I appreciate this," "You did a great job," "This was just what we needed," "Thanks for coming through on this last-minute request."

Praise costs nothing. It can mean a lot. If your employees are crushing it, thank them.

Strategies for Giving Recognition

If you are not accustomed to giving employees positive feedback, make it a regular habit by putting a "+" on your Outlook calendar every Tuesday

---

[23] https://benefitnews.com/news/workers-willing-to-leave-a-job-if-not-praised-enough

[24] https://benefitnews.com/news/workers-willing-to-leave-a-job-if-not-praised-enough

[25] https://getapp.com/resources/ultimate-guide-for-rewards-and-recognition-program/#:~:text=A%202018%20study%20found%20that,curb%20your%20attrition%20rate%20significantly

and Thursday, reminding you that if you have not yet said "thank you" or given recognition to any employees, you need to up your game.

Do not let remote work become an excuse for not recognizing good work. If you have not directly seen projects meriting compliments, send all your employees a quick e-mail survey asking, "Who's doing great work?" and "Whom do you enjoy working with?" Then, you can up the employee's dopamine dose by saying, "this 'thank you' comes from your coworkers as well as me."

Employees vary in the recognition they value. Some appreciate a manager's heartfelt compliment, others prefer public praise, others prefer their immediate manager alerting senior leaders about the employee's "above and beyond" performance. If you want to learn what type of recognition matters most, just ask.

Regardless of how you recognize employee achievements, adhere to these guidelines:

1. Recognition needs to be honest and genuine. Insincere praise falls flat.
2. Be specific. It is better if you say, "It was a great idea to add graphics and an executive summary to that stakeholder report" than if you say, "good job."
3. Be timely.

Professional Development Retains Accountable Employees

Professional development serves as a tool to attract and retain employees and as well as a strategy to increase employee engagement, morale, and productivity. Ongoing education gives employees something to look forward to and makes them feel respected and valued.

According to the Better Buys analysis and review site, 92 percent of the 2,000 employees they surveyed stated that inadequate professional development was second only to compensation as a reason for leaving jobs.[26] According to another study, 86 percent of employees stated that they would change jobs if a new employer offered more options for training.[27]

---

[26] https://hrmorning.com/articles/career-development-in-demand/
[27] https://brandman.edu/news-and-events/blog/in-demand-professional-development-opportunities

The Harris Poll reveals similar findings, reporting that roughly 70 percent of the 1,400 full-time employees surveyed in 2020 stated they were "somewhat likely to leave their current company" to work for an organization with a stronger focus on training and development. One-third of respondents (34 percent) stated that they left a job in the past year because the employer lacked employee development options.[28]

According to LinkedIn's 2020 Workplace Learning Report, 94 percent of employees would stay at a company longer if it invested in their career development.[29] LinkedIn's research further revealed that roughly a quarter of Gen Z and Gen Ys report that learning is the number one thing that makes them happy at work. More than one in four (27 percent) of Gen Z and Gen Y employees state that the number one reason they would leave their jobs is because their employers did not provide opportunities to learn and grow.

Professional Development Strategies

Employers can satisfy employee development expectations by using a variety of no-cost and low-cost strategies.

1. Outline clear careers paths within your organization, giving employees a powerful incentive for staying. Identify specific milestones for achievement so that your employees can understand what they need to do and can better visualize a future in your organization.
2. Take a personalized interest by discussing your employees' career aspirations and expectations with them and explore ways to provide what they want.
3. Provide virtual training and continuous learning opportunities such as video lunch and learn sessions using internal or external guest speakers (remember that employee career development delivers a strong return on investment for your organization) or YouTube or TED Talks-based employee discussion groups.

---

[28] https://businessnewsdaily.com/15085-disconnect-employee-development.html

[29] https://linkedin.com/business/learning/blog/learning-and-development/the-linkedin-learning-2020-workplace-report-l-d-taking-the-stra

4. Provide your employees the time and flexibility to attend local, in-person, or virtual industry events.

5. Create and support a mentoring program, which benefits both the mentors and the mentored employees.

6. Cross-train employees and rotate employee roles. Not only does the human brain thrive with new learning and variety, but temporary assignments in different departments often opens the door to improving departmental teamwork; also, the brief hiatus from their daily tasks challenges and reinvigorates employees.

7. Train your supervisors to be great coaches. Coaching leads to a 62 percent higher level of employee engagement.[30]

8. Succession planning shows high-potential employees that you see them as evolving into your organization's future leaders.

9. "Stretch" assignments give employees the chance to learn while handling intriguing projects that provide them the skills, competencies, and confidence to apply for higher-level positions.

10. Job enrichment activities add depth, challenge, and excitement to an employee's current job through increased control and responsibility. Aim to integrate learning in every project so that employees are encouraged to dive in and learn by doing.

Retention Strategies a "Must" During the Pandemic

Crises like the COVID-19 global pandemic, or other natural or man-made disasters such as cyber-attacks, earthquakes, workplace violence, hurricanes, massive embezzlement, bankruptcy filing, and raging wildfires, force employers to play their retention "A" game.

Crises hit employees hard, producing high levels of uncertainty, stress, negative morale, homelife and financial problems, and workplace disruption. A crisis can make or break an organization, and many employees leave organizations after major changes or in anticipation of them. The critical factor: leadership. It takes leadership to keep an employee team

---

[30] https://hci.org/system/files/research//files/field_content_file/2016%2520ICF.pdf

positive, resilient, and forward-thinking when the employees' personal and professional lives teeter on the edge.

During crises, leaders need to:

- Work with their employees to take ownership of the disruption, creating a team that rallies behind the leader to "beat the chaos."
- Ask employees for their ideas to fully engage them in handling the crisis.
- Authentically empathize with your employees. Communicate that you know things are tough, but "we're in this together."
- Ensure your employees know their safety and health is your number one priority.
- Let your employees know you are there to support them, can offer flexibility if they need it, and intend to get them the resources they need to succeed in their jobs.
- Conduct regular "all hands" and "state of the organization" meetings to keep employees abreast of recent changes, well informed of concerning successes, and plans for addressing current challenges. These meetings offer as much predictability as is feasible and enable organizations to adapt and act with urgency.

CHAPTER 10

Tailoring Your Accountability Management Strategies to Gen X, Y, and Z

Chapter 10 provides you a framework for tailoring your accountability management strategies to members of Gen X, Y, and Z, who may not respond as well to traditional managerial strategies as did Baby Boomers. This means all managers, even Gen X and Y managers, need to up their game by adapting to employees of different generations.

Although individuals in each generation defy stereotypic generalizations, understanding the broad themes true of many in each generation helps business owners and managers best motivate and manage individuals from a different generation than their own.

Generational Truths

Each generation has its own personality, shaped by social, cultural, and political influences. Members of each generation view authority, respect, rules, right and wrong differently. They bring to the workforce different values and expectations.

To orient you to the generations, those in:

- Baby Boomers were born between 1944 and 1964.
- Gen Xers were born between 1965 and 1980.
- Gen Ys (or millennials) were born between 1981 and 1994.
- Gen Zs were born between 1995 and 2010.

Baby Boomers

If you are a Baby Boomer, born in the years after the Second World War ended, you were raised to believe in the American dream. You believe hard work pays off and rewards come to those who earn and deserve them. You want the good guy to win and the bad guy to lose by the end of the movie and feel ripped off when they do not. You probably remember where you were in 1963 when John Fitzgerald Kennedy was assassinated.

Gen X

Gen Xers, born between 1965 and 1980, experienced these shaping influences during their early years:

- The Vietnam war and its aftermath
- The Women's Liberation movement
- The birth of Tandy and Apple personal computers (1976);
- Watergate (1973)
- 66 American hostages held in Iran
- Ronald Reagan's inauguration

Gen X Characteristics

Gen Xers are independent, many having been raised as latch-key children. When they arrived home after school, they remained alone or with siblings for several hours before their parents returned. During these hours, they ate snacks; did homework (or not); played video games; and connected with their friends via instant messenger, text, Facebook, or other social media.

As a result, when they enter the workforce, they view Baby Boomers who hover or even check in too frequently as micro-managers. They want those above them to let go of the reins. This aligns well with your desire for them to show accountability, as you can give them a list of goals to accomplish and let them work the list.

Gen X wants credit for what they do and recognition for their contributions, along with positive and improvement-oriented feedback.

One unhappy Gen Xer complained to me that she received her cable bill more often than she received feedback from her boss even after she had made it clear how important his guidance was to her. Gen Xers want competitive compensation and benefits and performance-based rewards that reflect their individual performance in direct proportion to their achievement. Link accountability to achievement, and you have a win/win.

Gen Xers had an egalitarian and not a hierarchical relationship with their parents. In early schooling, Gen Xers were graded on their ability to challenge concepts and others. Because their Baby Boomer parents coddled them, they are accustomed to managers who treat them as valued team members.

The U.S. divorce rate tripled during a Gen Xer's formative years. Half of their parent's marriages ended in divorce. This appears to have changed their views concerning commitment. Gen Xers expect employers to invest in them in exchange for their making a commitment. They value training, opportunity, exposure to decision makers, and freedom to show their talents with the tangible results they create and for which they can take credit. As a result, the coaching and recognition you provide matters greatly to members of this generation.

For Gen Xers, earning respect and dues-paying at work are obsolete concepts because they feel entitled to respect. Employers engage them by discussing what they can learn and what their jobs and organizations can do for them. Gen Xers are not generally interested in traditional perks. In multiple surveys, Gen Xers ranked compensation less important than recognition, praise, opportunity to learn and to develop marketable skills, work/life balance, flexible work hours, and having fun at work.[1] A recent Gallup study reveals that training and development are significant attractors and retainers for Generation Xers, who value on-the-job education even more than Baby Boomers. The study documented that 80 percent of those surveyed considered the availability of training a major factor in choosing a new job.[2]

Gen X is techno-literate; they grew up with computers. They spend as much time conversing electronically as they do face to face; they are not

---

[1] Tulgan, B. 2000. *Managing Generation X.*
[2] Zemke, R., C. Raines, B. Filipczak. 2013. *Generations at Work.*

afraid to ask questions. They want to work in fast-moving organizations with access to the latest technology. Allow this generation to create systems where they can self-manage their projects. If you make their incentive package attractive and offer them the flexibility and professional development they seek, they will show accountability in the form of quick results.

Gen Y or Millennials

How would you finish the following statements?
"Patience is a _____".
"Good things come to those who _____".
If you answered "virtue" and "wait," you are not Gen Y. I asked my son and his Gen Y friends to finish those statements. They responded that patience is a mystery; those who are patient get run over, and good things come to those who go after and seize them.

Gen Ys, born between 1985 and 1994 experienced these shaping influences:

- MTV (1981)
- AIDS (1984)
- The Challenger space shuttle disaster (1986)
- The Internet becomes global (1989)
- The Persian Gulf war (1991); they saw it fought on television in their living room
- The Cold War's end (1992)
- O. J. Simpson's arrest (1994)

Gen Y or Millennial Characteristics

Gen Ys are the children of Baby Boomers (48 percent) and Gen Xers (52 percent). Their name fits well; many Gen Ys refuse to do "what" until they are given the "why." For this reason, the purpose discussions presented in Chapter 5 matter greatly.

If you manage Gen Ys, assume they have a microchip in their brain that filters out instructions until they are linked with "acceptable" reasons. In schools, Gen Ys were raised to challenge what was presented and to freely speak their minds. Unless you explain the "why" of goals and projects, they question "why should I do that?"; "what's in it for me if I listen?" and "can I trust what you say?" If you understand where Gen Y comes from, you will not take these questions personally.

Like Gen Xers, Gen Ys are latch-key kids. Of them, 50 percent come from single-parent homes; 80 percent of them have working mothers. Many Gen Ys grew up spending hours watching television or playing video games and grew up amid rapid, radical social change. This, along with the national and international turmoil in their formative years—children their own ages killed in schools and the September 11, 2001, terrorist attacks—have desensitized them.

Stimulus junkies, Gen Ys are wired for the here and now. They want instant feedback, immediate compensation, and rapid results. They do not believe "all this and more will be yours one day if you work hard."

This changes the game for employers. You cannot easily stir Gen Ys emotions with rah-rah motivational pep talks or expect them to be deeply affected by verbal warnings. Unless you prove to them why it benefits them, most Gen Ys do not expect to be in the same job a year from now or working for the same employer three years from now. They view job security and company loyalty as an oxymoron.

Unlike Baby Boomers who believe that hard work pays off, rewards come to those who deserve them, and the good guy wins by the end of the movie, Gen Ys have seen the bad guy get away with misdeeds too many times. They consider rules and consequences to be negotiable and may remind you that O. J. Simpson and Martha Stewart made more money after prison than before. Highly cynical, they respect the unvarnished truth. Imagine that they are thinking, "been there, done that, got the tee shirt."

All of the aforementioned have upsides as well. Gen Ys handle change easily, without being thrown off their course. As an employer, you will want to stay current with technology; involve them in new initiatives; throw interesting and challenging projects at them; and break free from using only hourly wage compensation. For Gen Ys, goals inspire when the employees get rewards immediately. Reward what you want to see, and they will quickly deliver.

Although Gen Y are techno-savvy and highly educated (the best educated group in history), their video-game upbringing and texting reliance results in them lacking the interpersonal and conflict-resolution skills of older generations. At the same time, Gen Ys hope to form friendships at the workplace and agree that human connections can make work fun. Chapter 6's team training provides you tools to address this need.

The flexibility options outlined in Chapter 8 hugely appeal to Gen Ys. According to a *Harvard Business Review* Study of more than 1,500 U.S. workers, Gen Ys report that the "normal" workday structure makes it challenging for them to make time for exercise and healthy living.[3]

According to recent LinkedIn surveys, roughly a quarter of Gen Ys and Gen Zs report that learning is the number one thing that makes them happy at work.[4] More than one in four (27 percent) employees state that the number one reason they would leave their jobs is because their employers did not provide opportunities to learn and grow. Evidence also exists that Gen Y/millennials rank the ability to learn and grow as their most important job consideration.[5]

Chapter 5's goal-setting, scorekeeping, and reward systems motivate Gen Y. Because they are wired to expect praise and want to be a "star," if you show them opportunity and a way to become a hero/heroine, they will work around the clock.

My own research and that of others reveals what Gen Ys want in a boss; that s/he:

- Has good management skills
- Is approachable, pleasant, and easy to get along with
- Is understanding and caring
- Is a good advisor and supporter
- Is flexible and open-minded
- Respects, values, and appreciates employees[6]

---

[3] https://hbr.org/2018/06/96-of-u-s-professionals-say-they-need-flexibility-but-only-47-have-it

[4] https://linkedin.com/business/learning/blog/learning-and-development/the-linkedin-learning-2020-workplace-report-l-d-taking-the-stra

[5] https://brandman.edu/news-and-events/blog/in-demand-professional-development-opportunities

[6] https://flexjobs.com/employer-blog/the-benefits-of-allowing-employees-a-flexible-schedule/

The coaching framework you learned in Chapter 9 and the expectation-setting presented in Chapter 5 stands you in good stead with Gen Ys. If you provide new Gen Y employees a clear, realistic picture of the work environment, spell out your expectations and goals; learn their goals, together you can define strategies that they can accountably use to meet those goals.

Generation Z

Born between 1996 and 2010 and 25.9 percent of the U.S. population, Gen Z breaks free from many of the patterns found in Gen Xers and Ys. Gen Z did not receive coddling from Baby Boomer parents. Parented by Gen Xers, Gen Zs watched their Gen Y siblings not make it in the outside world and come home to live with mom and dad to save on rent. Gen Zs want more for themselves, and as a result, give more to their employers.

What sets Gen Z apart:

- They grew up during the War on Terror
- Global warming and climate change are facts of life for them
- Severe economic recession clouded their childhood and teenage years
- COVID-19 throttled many of their career dreams

Gen Z Characteristics

Gen Zs grew up fast, in a climate of chaos, volatility, and uncertainty. They do not believe in the "American dream." Gen Zs are more realistic and independent than Gen Xers and Gen Ys, whose parents gave them everything they needed. They value straight talk and pragmatic realism and do not believe that anything is flawless or perfect.

Gen Z's are future-focused, unlike Gen Ys that are now-focused. Gen Zs are entrepreneurial; 72 percent of high school students want to start a business someday. Gen Zs are self-directed; they look for solutions on their own and do not rely on parents, teachers, or supervisors for explanations. Gen Zs will work for success, though they expect quick results and can be overconfident in their knowledge.

Gen Zs live online and share details of their personal and work lives across dozens of platforms. Digital natives, they are technologically savvy, have instant access to and quickly process mountains of data and crave constant and immediate feedback. They are multitaskers, use various media simultaneously, and value speed over accuracy. Gen Zs prefer the speed of texting to e-mail and have tremendous online collaboration skills.

The forces that impacted their childhood such as the War on Terror and climate change fears make them determined to make an impact by providing solutions to the world's problems. They are naturally oriented to accountability.

Their jobs are their identifiers. They want to use their minds, to make a significant contribution and desire challenging, meaningful work. If they cannot achieve this in their current job/organization, they will quickly move on. Gen Zs are multicultural and diverse; multiracial children are the fastest growing youth group, and this and political and cultural events orient them to social justice. Studies reveal that Gen Zs are motivated by opportunities for advancement (34 percent); more money (27 percent) and meaningful work (23 percent).[7]

Gen Zs expect managers to listen to their opinions and involve them in problem-solving and in decision-making meetings, and not leave them on the sidelines. They do not want to wait years for their opportunity. Employers can use a Gen Z's desire for independence, autonomy, and self-directedness by giving them tasks and projects and expecting them to produce. Spell out what they are accountable for and let them go to work. Tap into a Gen Z's entrepreneurial spirit by giving them the freedom to make products and services "their own."

Conclusion: Accountability Is a Game Changer

Accountability can be a game changer for you and your organization. Accountability offers a concrete reality that aligns with integrity, forms a foundation for trust, and powers results.

---

[7] https://flexjobs.com/employer-blog/the-benefits-of-allowing-employees-a-flex-ible-schedule/

Now, more than ever, we need accountability at all levels in our organizations as we create not just a new normal but a better normal. Accountability gives leaders that embrace it the competitive advantage they need to achieve unparalleled success.

Managing for Accountability gives you a roadmap for creating that better normal. The tools you have received form the basis for creating an outstanding organization one employee at a time. As you have learned each time you have implemented the pragmatic strategies presented, accountability delivers tangible employee and organization-changing outcomes.

Accountable employees demonstrate ownership, investing themselves in your organization as well as their careers. They do what they say they will and more. They show initiative, tackle obstacles, and communicate candidly with you and each other.

You have learned how to attract the highest-quality job applicants and how to sift through stacks of resumes to identify the candidates that will take responsibility for results and demonstrate resilience even when the going gets tough.

You have learned how to orient new employees to integrate into your organization and quickly attain competency. You have developed the strong coaching relationships with your employees that ensure continued honest two-way communication and continued performance improvement.

You have acquired field-tested strategies to inspire every employee to fully commit to your organization and to "own" their jobs and the goals you mutually seek. In addition to setting expectations for accountability as part of your organization's culture, if any of your employees backtrack, you know exactly how to press the reset button and realign them.

Through implementing the team-development exercises, you have built high-performing, highly accountable teams that can transform your organization into one that seamlessly executes your vision.

In addition to fostering accountability at all levels in your organization, you have committed to yourself as a proactive, accountable leader. With accountability integral to your core and your organization, you can create a better normal for your organization.

I urge you to keep *Managing for Accountability* handy as a reference tool for handling new and challenging situations as they arise and to share it with the managers on your team.

Thank you for taking this journey into accountability with me.

Bibliography

Arbinger Institute. 2018. *Leadership and Self-deception.*

Arbinger Institute. 2019. *The Outward Mindset: Seeing Beyond Ourselves.*

Baney, D. 2017. *The 3x5 Coach: A Practical Guide to Coaching.*

Cohen, M. 2006. *What You Accept Is What You Teach: Setting Standards for Employee Accountability.* Creative Health Care Management.

Connors, R., and T. Smith. 2016. *The Wisdom of Oz: Using Personal Accountability to Succeed in Everything You Do.*

Connors, R., and T. Smith. 2009. *How Did That Happen: Holding People Accountable for Results the Positive Principled Way.*

Connors, R., and T. Smith. 2012. *Change the Culture, Change the Game: The Breakthrough Strategy for Energizing Your Organization and Creating Accountability for Results.*

Connors, R., T. Smith, and C. Hickman. 2010. *The Oz Principle: Getting Results Through Individual & Organizational Accountability.*

Connors, R., T. Smith, C. Hickman, T. Skousen, and M. Nicolls. 2016. *Fixit: Getting Accountability Right: 240 Solutions to your Toughest Business Problem.*

Corbridge, T., J. Jones, C. Hickman, and T. Smith. 2019. *Propeller: Accelerating Change by Getting Accountability Right.*

Curry, L. 2006 and 2014. *Solutions.* Communication Works, Inc.

Doerr, J. 2018. *Measure What Matters: How Google, Bono, and the Gates Foundation Rock the World with OKRs.*

Gostick, A., and C. Elton. 2012. *All In: How the Best Managers Create a Culture of Belief and Drive Big Results.*

LaBorde, G. 1987. *Influencing with Integrity: Management Skills for Communication and Negotiation.* West Wales: Crown House Publishing.

Miller, J. 2005. *Flipping the Switch: Unleash the Power of Personal Accountability Using the QBQ!.* New York, NY: Penguin Random House.

Miller, J. 2004. *QBQ! The Question Behind The Question.* New York, NY: Penguin Random House.

Melena, S. 2018. *Supportive Accountability: How to Inspire People and Improve Performance.* La Mesa, CA: Melena Consulting Group.

Patterson, K., J. Grenny, R. McMillan, and A. Switzler. 2002. *Crucial Conversations Tools for Talking When Stakes Are High.* New York, NY: McGraw-Hill Education.

Patterson, K. 2013. *Crucial Accountability: Tools for Resolving Violated Expectations, Broken Commitments, and Bad Behavior.* New York, NY: McGraw-Hill Education.

Phillips, J., and A. Connell. 2011. *Managing Employee Retention: A Strategic Accountability*. Abingdon, Oxfordshire: Routledge.

Sinek, S. 2009. *Start with Why: How Great Leaders Inspire Everyone to Take Action*. New York, NY: Portfolio/Penguin.

Tulgan, B. 2000. *Managing Generation X: How to Bring Out the Best in Young Talent*. New York, NY: W.W. Norton Company.

Voss, C. 2016. *Never Split the Difference: Negotiating As If Your Life Depended on It*. New York, NY: Harper Business.

Willink, J., and L. Babin. 2018. *The Dichotomy of Leadership*. New York, NY: St. Martin's Press.

Willink, J., and L. Babin. 2015. *Extreme Ownership: How U.S. Navy Seals Lead and Win*. New York, NY: St. Martin's Press.

Zemke, R., C. Raines, and B. Filipczak. 2013. *Generations at Work*. New York, NY: AMACOM.

About the Author

Lynne Curry, PhD, is the President of Communication Works, Inc. (Anchorage, Alaska), the Founder of www.workplacecoachblog.com, and was the Founder and CEO of The Growth Company, Inc., a nationally respected management consulting company she started in 1978 and sold in 2017. Lynne grew her company to be one in which her employees aligned with the company's mission and vision—and she has taught field-tested accountability skills and strategies to business owners, executives, managers, and supervisors.

Curry has directly worked with more than 4,300 organizations in Washington, Oregon, California, Alaska, Hawaii, Connecticut, Arizona, Michigan, Washington D.C., Illinois, New York, Arizona, Colorado, Texas, Japan, Korea, China, Guam, and England. Her clients have included the World Bank, the U.S. Department of Defense, Conoco Phillips, and British Petroleum.

Curry has qualified in court as an expert witness in the areas of management best practices, HR, and workplace issues.

Curry's weekly blog, www.workplacecoachblog.com, has more than 2,000 subscribers from 89 countries.

Curry is the author of *Beating the Workplace Bully: A Tactical Guide to Taking Charge* (AMACOM 2016). Curry has authored three earlier books: *Won By One* (Communication Works 1996), *Managing Equally and Legally* (McFarland & Company, 1990), and *Solutions* (2006 and 2014 Communication Works). Lynne is the author of Love.com, a novel featuring a workplace setting based on her extensive HR experience.

Curry is on the Editorial Advisory Board for Plain Language Media and publishes a monthly column in both Law Office Manager and Medical Office Manager.

In addition, Curry has published hundreds of articles in print and online media, including inc.com, sheknows.com, workingwomen.com, and U.S. News & World Report. Lynne began publishing when she was eight years old (in her hometown newspaper).

Curry has written a weekly Dear Abby of the Workplace newspaper column for 39 years (adn.com) in newspapers in Alaska, Washington, and Illinois.

Curry has been interviewed on radio shows and stations such as the Voice of America, KBYK, KSKA, and KNBA on topics such as "Resolving Workplace Conflicts" and "Outsmarting Workplace Bullies." Curry has been interviewed on Monster.com podcasts, as well as on television stations ABC/FOX, KTUU, and KTVA.

Lynne served as the Chair for Alaska's Labor Relations Agency under two governors.

Curry has a doctorate in social psychology from Union Graduate School-West, a Senior Professional in Human Resources certificate from the Human Resources Certification Institute, and a Senior Certified Professional Certificate from the Society for Human Resource Management.

Curry has three children, Ben, Jenny, and Joey; three grandchildren, MaHayla, Cooper, and Parker, and two collies that she hikes with daily, Zeke and Gabriel.

Index

OTHER TITLES IN THE HUMAN RESOURCE MANAGEMENT AND ORGANIZATIONAL BEHAVIOR COLLECTION

- *Emotional Connection: The EmC Strategy* by Lola Gershfeld and Ramin Sedehi
- *Civility at Work* by Lewena Bayer
- *Lean on Civility* by Christian Masotti and Lewena Bayer
- *Leaderocity* by Richard Dool
- *Agility* by Michael Edmondson
- *Strengths Oriented Leadership* by Matt L. Beadle
- *Leadership In Disruptive Times* by Sattar Bawany
- *The Successful New CEO* by Christian Muntean
- *Level-Up Leadership* by Michael J. Provitera
- *Chief Kickboxing Officer* by Alfonso Asensio
- *Transforming the Next Generation Leaders* by Sattar Bawany
- *Breakthrough* by Saundra Stroope
- *Women Leaders* by Sapna Welsh and Caroline Kersten
- *The New World of Human Resources and Employment* by Tony Miller

Concise and Applied Business Books

The Collection listed above is one of 30 business subject collections that Business Expert Press has grown to make BEP a premiere publisher of print and digital books. Our concise and applied books are for...

- Professionals and Practitioners
- Faculty who adopt our books for courses
- Librarians who know that BEP's Digital Libraries are a unique way to offer students ebooks to download, not restricted with any digital rights management
- Executive Training Course Leaders
- Business Seminar Organizers

Business Expert Press books are for anyone who needs to dig deeper on business ideas, goals, and solutions to everyday problems. Whether one print book, one ebook, or buying a digital library of 110 ebooks, we remain the affordable and smart way to be business smart. For more information, please visit www.businessexpertpress.com, or contact sales@businessexpertpress.com.

www.ingramcontent.com/pod-product-compliance
Lightning Source LLC
Chambersburg PA
CBHW061313220326
41599CB00026B/4858